Vi.

SOU'.

& COSTA DEL SOL

## Other MPC Visitor's Guides of Interest:

1 Costa Brava to Costa Blanca
2 Northern & Central Spain
3 Mallorca, Menorca, Ibiza & Formentera
4 Portugal

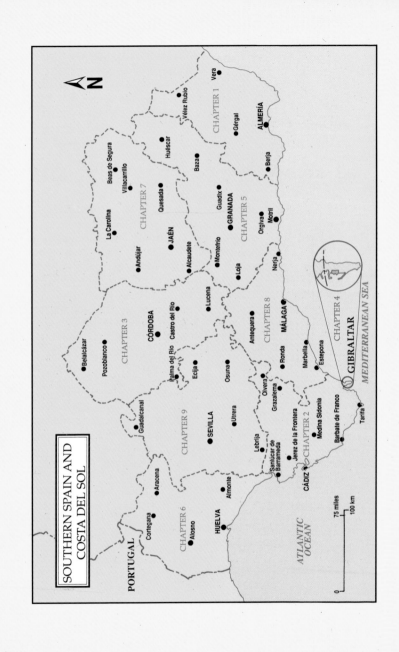

# VISITOR'S GUIDE

# SOUTHERN SPAIN
## & COSTA DEL SOL

## Barbara Mandell

MPC

Published by:
Moorland Publishing Co Ltd,
Moor Farm Road West, Ashbourne,
Derbyshire DE6 1H, England

ISBN 0 86190 536 9

1st edition 1990
2nd revised edition 1994
Reprinted 1995

British Library Cataloguing in Publication Data:
A catalogue record for this book is available from the British Library.

Colour Origination by J. Film Process, Singapore

Printed in Hong Kong byWing King Tong Co Ltd

Front cover : *Casares* (MPC Picture Collection)
Rear cover: *Fuengirola* (MPC Picture Collection)
Title page: *Ronda* (MPC Picture Collection)

Illustrations have been supplied as follows: MPC Picture Collection: pp 11,
46 (both), 63 (both), 70 (top), 71 (both), 118, 119 (both), 126 (both), 127
(both), 130, 131 (both), 134, 135 (both), 138, 139 (both), 142, 143, 146 (both),
147, 159 (bottom), 162 (top); Spanish National Tourist Office: p 75 (top).
All other illustrations were supplied by the author.

# *CONTENTS*

## Key to Symbols Used in Text Margin and on Maps

 Recommended walk

 Archaeological site

 Nature reserve/Animal interest

 Garden

 Cave

Skiing facilities

 Church/Ecclesiastical site

 Building of interest

 Castle/Fortification

 Museum/Art gallery

 Beautiful view/Scenery, Natural phenomenon

 Other place of interest

 Watersports

## Key to Maps

—— Main road

═══ Motorway

 River

 Town/City

● Town/Village

 Lake

------ Province Boundary

—·— Country Boundary

## Note On The Maps

The maps drawn for each chapter while comprehensive are not designed to be used as route maps but rather to locate main towns, villages and places of interest.

# INTRODUCTION

A ndalucía, the *Al-Andalus* of the Moors, is a region of contradictions and superlatives. It has the highest mountains in
Spain, perpetual snow almost within sight of an isolated pocket of
semi-desert and one of the most extensive marshland nature reserves in Europe. The shoreline varies from long uninterrupted
stretches of golden sand to slithers of grey, often pebble-covered,
beaches festooned with coloured umbrellas and sun worshippers.

There are ancient cities and high-rise holiday resorts, crumbling
castles, modern highways, prehistoric caves, hills intricately patterned with olive groves and atmospheric villages clinging like
white limpets to high outcrops of bare, forbidding rock. It is a land
of rags and riches, of ancient cultures and of bloodshed and atrocities, of exuberant carnivals and sad, haunting melodies, which plays
host to millions of holidaymakers every year but is known to few of
them. Travellers undoubtedly see more than tourists but even they
know that it takes years to do more than scratch the surface of
Andalucía.

Geographically the region occupies a large percentage of Southern
Spain, from the Río Guadiana, which marks the border with Portugal, to Murcia, looking out eastwards across the Mediterranean. It
consists of eight provinces — Huelva, Cádiz, Málaga, Granada and
Almería along the coast with Sevilla, Córdoba and Jaén inland to the
north of them. Apart from Portugal and Murcia its immediate
neighbours are Extremadura, the home of the Conquistadores who
opened up large areas of the New World in the sixteenth century, and
the provinces of Ciudad Real and Albacete, which form part of
Castilla-La Mancha. Its most impressive mountain range is the Sierra
Nevada, the highest section of the Baetic Cordillera that runs along
the Mediterranean coast and gives birth to the Guadalquivir which

rises in the uplands of the Sierra de Cazorla.

Everything seems to grow in Andalucía from maize and cereals to almonds and olives, with vineyards, rice fields, citrus orchards and intensely cultivated market gardens. Black fighting bulls are raised on the southern plains whereas goat herds climb slowly up and down the hillsides with their noisy flocks. Pig farmers in the area are said to produce the best ham in Spain but fish are even more plentiful. There are mineral deposits and light industry, but for visitors the local crafts are much more interesting, especially leather, lace, woven articles and wrought iron work.

The weather in Andalucía varies almost as much as the scenery. The coastal belt has mild winters with some rain and occasionally a spectacular thunderstorm when heavy seas can cause damage to shoreline promenades. The summers are hot and sometimes oppressive. The inland areas suffer even more extremes with bitter winters and summers that have been described as furnaces. But in spring and autumn bright sunshine is counteracted by cool breezes and early almond blossom throws a soft pink haze over the countryside, to be replaced by the harsher gold of gorse and mimosa. As the year draws to a close the plains to the north ripple under a gigantic blanket of cereal crops, ripe and ready for harvesting.

The population is scattered very unevenly across the region, being concentrated for the most part in historic centres like Sevilla, Granada, Cádiz and Córdoba and along the Costa del Sol from Estepona to Nerja and beyond. Occasionally the smaller towns of the interior prove to be somewhat larger than expected. A case in point is Jaén, where the massive castle-turned-*parador* gazes down on the capital far below. Then there is Ronda with its gaping chasm and Arcos, isolated high up on a rocky spur. The villages come in varying shades of white and are frequently clustered round an ancient fortress that may be little more than an empty shell. Much of the land is made up of vast estates where the introduction of modern methods and machinery has reduced the labour force, leaving poverty and migration in its wake. Some people believe that Spain's entry into the Common Market will reverse this trend but others have still to be convinced.

Andalucía, like the rest of Spain, is predominantly Catholic, born out by its large and sometimes over-opulent churches and by the number of religious celebrations held throughout the whole area. These can be modest pilgrimages, undertaken by the faithful in order to pay their respects to the Virgin in some isolated sanctuary, or massive annual events such as the fiesta at El Rocío when a million or more people converge on the small village which hardly sees a single visitor at other times of the year. Holy Week is marked by solemn and sumptuous processions in places like Sevilla, whereas Carnival has no religious connections apart, perhaps, from a tenuous link with the gods of Ancient Rome. The many other fairs and festivals are just as well attended. They are every bit as colourful, noisy and exuberant and include anything from folklore to flowers and fireworks.

Traditional costumes tend to be flamboyant and extremely becoming. The same love of colour and geometric design is apparent in many local dishes and flavours are equally unpredictable. Some of the best Spanish wines come from Andalucía and especially from Jerez, where they were popular with the Greeks in the fourth century BC, long before the English referred to them as sherry.

Each successive era has left its indelible mark on Andalucía. The Serranía de Ronda has its prehistoric cave dwellings decorated with rock paintings while Antequera is known, among other things, for its burial chambers dating from 2500BC. The Vandals and the Visigoths made short work of most of the improvements introduced by the Romans, although an occasional aqueduct has survived, augmented by one or two ruins including *Itálica*, near Sevilla, and the remains of *Baelo Claudia* on the Atlantic coast west of Tarifa. The Moors, on the other hand, had a profound influence on the architecture of the entire region from remote hill villages to world famous buildings such as the mosque at Córdoba, the Alhambra in Granada, Sevilla's Giralda Tower and, somewhat less widely known, the castles of Málaga and Almería.

In due course a new form, known as Mudejár, developed which proved to be a happy marriage of Romanesque, Gothic and Islamic art, personified by the Alcázar in Sevilla. Later the Italian Renaissance influenced several architects such as Andrés de Vandelvira who designed the cathedral in Jaén and the captivating town of Úbeda. Baroque was responsible for a sometimes rather indigestible outbreak of elaborate decoration before it was overtaken by a swing back to simpler, more classical styles.

In the realms of art and music the region has just as much to offer. The illustrated manuscripts of the tenth century and the later wall paintings, used to decorate many of the churches, were supplanted by giant altarpieces. During the Golden Age the Sevilla School was made famous by men of the calibre of Murillo, Zurbarán and Alfonso Cano while one of the most famous names of the twentieth century is undoubtedly Picasso who was born in Málaga. Foreign composers drew on Andalucía for inspiration, among them Bizet for his opera *Carmen*, to be rivalled by their Spanish counterparts such as Manuel de Falla with works like *The Three-cornered Hat* and *Nights in the Gardens of Spain*.

Although none of Andalucía's many writers achieved the international status of Cervantes with his *Don Quixote*, Federico Garcia Lorca is now recognised as one of Spain's most outstanding poets and dramatists. It was left to the American authors Washington Irving and Ernest Hemingway to draw the attention of people everywhere to the romance and colour of the region through best sellers like *Tales of the Alhambra*, *For Whom the Bell Tolls* and *Death in the Afternoon*.

## HISTORY

The history of Spain is as long, as varied, as complicated and as bloodthirsty as any in Europe; and much of it started in Andalucía. Neanderthal man made his home in the area some 50,000 years ago and was succeeded in rapid succession by other prehistoric residents before the Iberians put in an appearance, probably around 7000BC. By 1100BC the Phoenicians and the Greeks had become regular visitors and were setting up trading posts along the coast, among them *Gades*, now known as Cádiz. They were ousted by the Carthaginians but when Hannibal set out for Italy via France with his famous elephants the Romans moved in to take their place.

Córdoba was established as an administrative centre in 151BC but it was another two centuries before the last pocket of local resistance was wiped out in the far north of the peninsula. Thereafter life went on more or less peacefully and even the introduction of Christianity gave no inkling of the atrocities to be perpetrated in its name during the long, dark centuries ahead.

The Visigoths and the Vandals created very little of any consequence because they were mostly hell bent on destruction. Although Andalucía survived these invasions and occupations rather better than the rest of the country the arrival of the Moors in 711 proved to be a blessing in disguise. The Muslims were both intelligent and tolerant and under Abd ar-Rahman, the first Emir of Al-Andalus, the cities of Córdoba, Málaga and Sevilla grew and prospered until eventually they surpassed every other centre in Western Europe. The best of Rome mingled with the best of Islam to reach new heights of art and architecture, wealth and scholarship.

However, like the Romans, the Muslims were determined to extend their frontiers but were much less efficient in this respect. They pushed northwards into France, were defeated in 732 and retired back across the Pyrénées where they were constantly at war with the local Christians and bedevilled by Arab-Berber rivalries in

*Sohail Castle at Fuengirola is one of the many reminders of
Andalucía's rich history*

the south. The Caliphat of Córdoba, founded in 929, started to
disintegrate after the loss of Toledo in 1085 when an appeal to the
Almoravids of North Africa brought reinforcements flooding across
the straits. Christian Spain mobilised under the banner of Alfonso
VII, Córdoba was captured in 1236, Sevilla fell 12 years later and by
the end of the century Granada was the only Moorish kingdom left
in Andalucía. However it was 1492 before the city was recovered by
the Catholic Monarchs, Ferdinand and Isabel. The marriage of these
two determined rulers united the kingdoms of Castile and Aragon
and created a partnership that was to unify the whole of Spain,
provide it with a mighty empire but, at the same time, plunge it into
iniquity.

Nearer home the Catholic Monarchs married their daughter Juana
to Philip the Fair, son of the Holy Roman Emperor, Maximilian of
Austria, in 1496. This was done mainly to provide themselves with
as many allies as possible in their opposition to France. In 1504
Gonzalo de Córdoba, better known as El Grand Capitán, captured

the kingdom of Naples for Isabel, but she died at about the same time and 2 years later Philip was also dead. Juana went mad and spent the rest of her life in a convent, leaving Ferdinand to act as regent for his grandson Charles, who had also inherited Burgundy and the Netherlands from his father. After Ferdinand's death in 1516 Charles returned to Spain to claim his kingdom which included Naples, Sardinia, Sicily and all the Spanish possessions overseas. Charles I also gathered in Austria and parts of Germany when he succeeded Maximilian and, without too much trouble, was acknowledged as the Holy Roman Emperor, Charles V.

The reign of the Habsburgs marked the beginning of the end for Spain. Charles V was constantly at war, mainly with France, although he found time to sack Rome, take Pope Clement VII prisoner and to capture Milan. He was forced to come to terms with Protestant Germany and put down revolts in Spain where his subjects objected to paying in men and money for his foreign expeditions. Finally he abdicated in favour of his son Philip II and retired to the monastery of Yuste, in Extremadura, where he died in 1558.

Philip II was no improvement. His religious mania gave full reign to the Inquisition, the Low Countries went a long way towards achieving their independence and his attempt to invade England after the death of his second wife, Mary Tudor, resulted in the loss of the Armada. The subject nations of the New World were treated just as badly as anyone at home who was found to have a trace of either Jewish or Moorish blood or showed the slightest leaning towards Protestantism. Hatred and resentment were rife everywhere and his successors had neither the wit nor the wisdom to prevent the country sliding into decay and bankruptcy. Of course there was an occasional victory, such as the Battle of Lepanto against the Turks and annexation of Portugal. However, by the time Charles II (the last of the Habsburgs) died in 1700, most of the Spanish possessions in Europe were back in the hands of their rightful owners.

The demise of the Habsburgs brought no respite for Spain. Charles died childless and willed his crown to the Duke of Anjou while Emperor Leopold renounced his rights to the throne in favour of his son, Archduke Charles of Austria. The rest of Europe decided that it had its own particular axes to grind and the War of Succession was joined. The ensuing battles favoured first one side and then the other but the Bourbons eventually came out on top and in 1714 Philip V was recognised as King of Spain. For the rest of the eighteenth century the country dabbled rather half-heartedly in foreign affairs such as the American War of Independence, but the only result of this was the sale of Florida to the newly-formed Republic in 1819.

Meanwhile Napoleon had become Emperor of France and persuaded the Spanish to join forces in the war against Britain. It was an unhappy alliance from the beginning. The country ceased to be a naval power when much of its fleet was destroyed, along with the French, at the Battle of Trafalgar. After the Aranjuez Revolt in 1808, Napoleon arrested Ferdinand VII and his father Charles, who had been forced to abdicate in his favour, and installed Joseph Bonaparte as King of Spain. The country did not take kindly to this new state of affairs and decided once again that force was the only remedy. In this they were ably assisted by the British under Wellington until Napoleon's abdication in 1814 put an end to the Peninsular War.

Ferdinand was returned to the throne but rivalries and insurrections once more brought the nation to its knees. Would-be monarchs jostled for possession of the crown and by the end of the nineteenth century all the overseas colonies had regained their independence, although northern Morocco became a Spanish Protectorate in 1912. Spain remained neutral during World War I but its internal troubles were even more acute than they had been before. In 1931 Alfonso XIII went into voluntary exile in the hope of averting a national catastrophy but by that time the outcome was inevitable.

After the outbreak of hostilities in 1936 General Francisco Franco landed in Andalucía at the head of a well-trained army of Moorish troops and soon captured the eastern part of the region including Extremadura. However a sizeable proportion of the army remained loyal to the government and the stage was set for a long and bitter civil war. Italy, Portugal and Germany sent aeroplanes and troops to help the insurgents, the Communists retaliated by organising the International Brigade and Britain and France opted for a policy of appeasement. One town after another fell to the Nationalists, although there was little action in Andalucía after Málaga was captured early in 1937. In January 1939 the Germans took Barcelona, Britain and France recognised the Franco regime in February and a month later Madrid and Valencia capitulated.

The years that followed were far from easy. The country was impoverished, old hatreds died hard and even Spain's neutrality in World War II was somewhat unconvincing. However, in 1953 Franco reached an agreement with the USA, exchanging military bases for much needed dollars and matters started to improve. After looking round for a successor, Franco decided to restore the monarchy in the person of Juan Carlos, the grandson of Alfonso XIII, who he considered to be suggestible enough to step into his shoes. However, the young king had other ideas and possessed both the character and the ability to see them through. Following his accession in 1975 he eased the country back on to democratic lines with the help of men like Adolfo Suarez. There were free elections for the first time in more than 30 years, the new liberal constitution of 1978 created a federal state on the lines of West Germany and an attempted coup by a section of the army in 1981 fizzled out on the orders of Juan Carlos.

With the return to normality Spain had started to pull itself up by its boot straps. Industrial enterprises were encouraged, large areas were irrigated, agriculture became more efficient and a determined effort was made to improve road and rail communications. Suddenly the coastal regions became a Mecca for tourists who at times outnumbered the total population of the country. Modest fishing villages found themselves transformed into hurriedly developed holiday resorts and the hillsides overlooking the Mediterranean broke out in a rash of Moorish-style villas, apartment blocks, neon signs and advertisements. Naturally, like any other country, Spain still has its problems, such as high unemployment, but with advantages like its membership of the EEC and an enlightened administration the future looks brighter than at any time since its famous Golden Age.

## ACCOMMODATION
Andalucía provides all types of accommodation to suit every individual taste and pocket. The *paradores* are state run establishments which guarantee a certain standard of service and comfort. Some are housed in ancient palaces, castles or convents with furnishings to match their surroundings, excellent restaurants and all the expected amenities. Others are modern and generally well-equipped. On a par with the *paradores* there are a number of first class hotels, especially in the main holiday resorts, but with a few five or four star examples further inland. Further down the scale most three star hotels and hostels have lifts, rooms with private baths and restaurants on the premises but they may be short of garages and parking facilities. Anything in the lower brackets can be very basic, providing little apart from a bed for the night. The advertised price is the cost of the room, not per person, and an extra charge is usually made for a continental breakfast.

Furnished accommodation covers just as wide a range as hotels and hostels. It is possible to rent fully-equipped luxury villas with swimming pools, gardens, beautiful views and regular staff. The less expensive variety may well have a pool, a sun terrace and perhaps maid service but in the lower price brackets it is useful to know what is included for the price. The same applies to furnished apartments which may be large and excellently equipped or hardly more than small studios with all the basic requirements but not much else besides. There are plenty of campsites all along the coast but comparatively few acceptable ones in the interior apart from those on the outskirts of some of the larger towns.

## CAFÉS, BARS AND RESTAURANTS

These come in all shapes and sizes, from the expensive, international variety to wayside inns and little bars. The first category are indistinguishable from those in any other country whereas the latter differ every bit as much as they do anywhere else. For the average holiday-maker it is always a good idea to choose somewhere that is full of local people, and sample the traditional dishes, rather than search for a deserted terrace with menus in three or four different languages. The best way of finding out about the various specialities is to visit a *tapas* bar where small quantities of a great many different dishes are served with the drinks. By having a *porción* (small helping) it is possible to try quite a few of them, after which anyone who is still hungry can order a *ración* (larger portion) of one that has proved to be especially appetising. However, visitors who are determined not to eat anything out of the ordinary will find plenty of familiar dishes in dozens of little cafés that cater for tourists in the major holiday centres. One of the advantages of *tapas* bars and cafés is that they are open all day and will supply something to eat at almost any time. The Spaniards themselves prefer to linger over lunch at around 1.30pm or 2pm, pop into a bar when the sun goes down and start thinking about dinner at 10pm or 11pm. However there is an increasing tendency for restaurants to open at 8.30pm or 9pm to accommodate their foreign visitors. Unless the bill states otherwise a service charge has not been included so a tip should always be added to the total.

## FAIRS, FÊTES AND FESTIVALS

Andalucía rejoices in some of the most colourful and emotive celebrations to be encountered anywhere. A large percentage are religious events. The most important of these are during Semana Santa (Holy Week), Corpus Christi and the Assumption of the Virgin while nearly every patron saint has a special day. In addition to this there are numerous pilgrimages, by far the largest of which is to El Rocio, in Huelva, at Whitsun. Events with a certain religious content include the Cavalcade of the Three Kings in January and the Crosses of May at the beginning of the month. In many cases these are overshadowed by annual events like Carnival in Cádiz and elsewhere, the Spring Fair in Sevilla, the Burial of the Sardine along the coast and the re-enactment of ancient battles between the Moors and the Christians. Finally there are flamenco festivals, concerts, theatres, special Goya bullfights in Ronda and ballet performances in the Nerja caves.

## FOOD AND DRINK

Most traditional dishes are common to all the different provinces of Andalucía although individual areas may have their own special ingredients and methods of cooking them. *Gazpacho* is a case in point, a delicious cold soup, probably at its best in Córdoba but served with endless variations elsewhere. Fried fish is another popular example which varies considerably between Cádiz and Málaga but grilled sardines are uniformly tasty on beaches up and down the coast. The seafood is excellent everywhere, especially red bream with onions or paprika in Huelva, all types of shellfish and molluscs in Cádiz, baby anchovies fried and piled up on a plate, justifying their name 'Foam of the Sea' in Málaga and tiny clams in Rincón de la Victoria. *La tortilla sacromonte* is a special festive omelette that owes its existance to the gypsies of Granada whereas *huevos a la flamenca*, consisting of eggs cooked on a bed of diced ham and vegetables, originated in Sevilla. Other things to look out for are spinach in Jaén, ox-tail, kidneys cooked in sherry and ham from Trevélez, said to be the best in Spain.

Although Andalucía produces several different kinds of wine the most famous are undoubtedly the sherries from Jerez which were known and appreciated by the Greeks in the fourth century BC. Córdoba wines from the Montilla mountains are light and dry with a high alcohol content while Málaga contributes a much darker variety known as *moscatel*, rather more akin to an apéritif.

## SPORTS AND PASTIMES

Because the coastal areas of Andalucía number their annual visitors in millions the main resorts make a feature of their various sports and entertainments. At the same time several inland regions are becoming increasingly aware of their potential and are introducing such things as riding holidays up in the mountains.

### Climbing and Potholing

There are certainly plenty of opportunities but at the moment these are individual pursuits rather than organised activities. It would be most unwise to set out on a holiday of this kind without making provision for any possible accidents or unexpected problems.

### Cycling

This is not really a national pastime as most Spaniards prefer motor cycles but there are some bicycles for hire along the coast. The hot summers and steep gradients would make a holiday like this both very demanding and extremely tiring.

## Fishing

This is a very popular sport throughout the region. There are well stocked lakes and rivers and plenty of trout in the mountain streams. Underwater fishing is possible nearly everywhere along the coast but the most ideal conditions are generally agreed to be in the Cabo de Gata area of Almería. Fishing boats can be hired for off-shore expeditions with some shark fishing near the Straits of Gibraltar. The necessary licences are obtainable from any of the provincial head-quarters of the National Institute for the Conservation of Nature (ICONA). Applications should give the name, address and passport number of the person concerned and include a cheque for the appropriate amount, drawn on one of the local banks. A detailed brochure *Fishing in Spain* is available from tourist offices.

## Golf

Golf is more a way of life than a recreation on the Costa del Sol. There are a few golf courses elsewhere, usually in the vicinity of a provin-cial capital, but the majority are strung out in an almost unbroken line from Nerja, on the border with Granada, to Sotogrande in Cádiz. At the moment a few to the east of Málaga city are 9-hole courses but the remainder have 18 holes. Most are open throughout the year and have equipment for hire, but it is an expensive sport in Andalucía.

## Hunting and Shooting

The Spaniards have always been addicted to hunting and shooting but nowadays there are certain rules and regulations which must be observed. Some birds and animals, such as eagles and lynx, are protected species, there are closed seasons which differ very little from year to year and certain types of guns are prohibited. Special permission is needed to hunt in the reserves, whether they are national or privately owned, but anyone can shoot over lands in common use provided they have the necessary licence and insurance cover. Licences can be obtained from the provincial headquarters of ICONA but it is also necessary to have a permit to import the relevant firearms. A brochure *Hunting in Spain* can be obtained from tourist offices and gives a great many useful details.

## Riding

Riding is very much a part of life in Spain with horses ranging from magnificent thoroughbreds to surefooted mountain ponies, mules and donkeys. There are riding stables which will arrange short outings or longer expeditions through mountains, donkey taxis in Mijas and even some donkey safaris. Spectator sports in this category include displays at the Andalucían Riding School and polo matches.

## Tennis

Tennis courts are very easy to find in Andalucía where most hotels with enough space have at least one, as well as rackets for hire. There are several tennis schools and the more modern urban developments often provide community courts for their residents.

## Walking

Andalucía is rather too mountainous for any but the most dedicated long distance walkers and hitchhiking, while not forbidden, is definitely frowned on. Very few Spaniards will try to thumb a lift, except in an emergency, and just as few motorists would think of offering one. However there are one or two places, such as El Torcal, near Antequera, where there are special paths signposted for visitors who would rather explore by themselves than accept the services of a guide.

## Water Sports

Water sports are the outstanding attraction all along the coast of Andalucía in addition to which there are some inland lakes and reservoirs where it is possible to sail, windsurf and swim. The most beautiful beaches are along the Costa de la Luz, in Huelva and Cádiz, whereas the most crowded are on the Costa del Sol. Here the sand is not nearly so inviting but there are more amenities such as beach restaurants, marinas, charter fleets and opportunities for water parachuting. Equipment can be hired and there are special schools where holidaymakers can learn to water ski, skin-dive or handle pleasure craft. Beach beds, umbrellas and all kinds of little inshore boats are available.

## Winter Sports

The Solynieve area of the Sierra Nevada is a very popular winter sports area where there is snow on the highest peaks all the year round. The majority of the hotels are open from November to May with cable cars, chair-lifts and ski-lifts to the upper slopes, a ski school and lessons from professional instructors during the season. Anyone wanting information about the weather or snow conditions should contact ☎ 22 75 00 in Granada or the automatic answering service up in the mountains on ☎ 48 02 42 or 48 01 53 (24 hours).

# 1

# *ALMERÍA*

---

Almería province may be said, with some justification, to suffer from a mild form of schizophrenia. On one hand it has a semi-desert region with dusty river beds, a lunar landscape and little evidence of any human habitation. On the other there is a sea of plastic sheeting, stretching almost as far as the eye can reach, protecting millions of healthy plants which have earned for themselves the title of the 'Vegetable Garden of Europe'. Several of the sandy beaches and isolated coves have not yet been discovered by the majority of tourists and holidaymakers although the capital and sprinkling of seaside resorts have a surprisingly high percentage of very presentable hotels and at least four first-rate ones.

Despite its generally arid appearance some areas of Almería have more in common with Europe than with North Africa. Inland from the capital there are citrus groves and vineyards producing lucious grapes, prehistoric caves and half forgotten villages where craftsmen live and work much as they have done for centuries. The region is bounded by Granada in the west and north, Murcia to the north and east, and has a Mediterranean coastline fractionally longer than those of its two neighbours put together. It is also the most easterly of the eight provinces of Andalucía.

Almería airport, on the road to Níjar, has regular flights to Madrid and Barcelona as well as to Melilla, the small Spanish toehold on the coast of Morocco which is also linked by a regular ferry service. Trains run every day to Madrid, Valencia and Barcelona and only less frequently to Córdoba and Sevilla. Buses shuttle to and from places as far apart as Algeciras and Tarragona, Jaén, Castellón and Cartagena with weekday schedules covering most of the province itself. As far as motorists are concerned there are three major roads, one from Murcia, the second from Granada and the third along the

19

coast from the Costa del Sol, with a selection of alternative routes, some of which are worth choosing for the scenery. At the bottom of the list come the inevitable short-cuts and byways, many of them better ignored unless you happen to be travelling by ox-cart or in a jeep.

The capital, **Almería** can be either hot and dusty or pleasantly warm and invigorating, depending on one's attitude and the time of year. It is probably at its best in the winter when the skies may occasionally be cloudy, giving a little rain, although the temperature seldom drops below 12°C (54°F). The port was known to both the Phoenicians and the Romans but it was the Moors who built its massive **Alcazaba** which still dominates the town. This impressive fortress is said to have been more powerful than any other in Spain but it was badly damaged by an earthquake in 1522 and the palace on the nearby hill of San Cristóbal has completely disappeared. A lot of time and effort has gone into repairing the curtain walls and towers, built by Abd-ar-Rahman II (the Caliph of Córdoba) but there is not a great deal to see inside. The second line of fortifications has given way to public gardens. Beyond them archaeologists have been at work on the site of the royal apartments adjoining the former mosque and a watch tower added by the Christians in the fifteenth century.

The old town, with its narrow streets and typical small houses, is clustered on the hillside below the castle walls. To the west is the Chanca, where most of the local fishermen have their homes, while the cathedral is a tidy walk away on the opposite side. This is a fairly ornate building dating from 1524 and standing on the site of an ancient mosque.

There are several small churches in the vicinity, among them the fifteenth-century Church of San Pedro which also replaced a former mosque and was largely rebuilt 200 years ago, and the Church of Santiago el Viejo, mostly original and now a national monument. Among the city's more modern attractions are a bullring, yacht club, some delightful shops and cafés on the tree-lined Avenida de Almería and an archaeological museum. There are two first class hotels in the capital, half a dozen comfortable ones and a sprinkling of less ambitious establishments as well as furnished apartments and a distant campsite.

On the far side of the Wall of Jayrán, the line of ramparts linking the Alcazaba with the non-existant palace on the Cerro de San Cristóbal, is the **Centro de Rescate de la Fauna Sahariana**. This ranch was established in 1971 with the help of the Worldwide Fund for Nature to rescue various species of animals, birds and reptiles normally resident in the Sahara but in grave danger of becoming extinct. The experiment has proved a resounding success. The area is not automatically open to the public but it is possible to get permission to visit the centre from its main office in the city.

The capital, like the rest of the province, is a great place for traditional celebrations of one kind or another. Holy Week is marked by solemn processions on Wednesday, Thursday and Good Friday. The last week of August is given over to fiestas which include everything from sporting events and exhibitions to bull fights, singing and dancing, and there are repeat performances of most of the events during the winter. These end on the first Sunday in January with a procession in honour of the Virgin of the Sea to the beach of Torre García.

For the benefit of anyone suffering from indigestion, an attack of nerves or twinges of rheumatism, there are the thermal waters of **Alhama de Almería**, a little spa in the Sierra Alhamilla. It has been a well known watering place since the Romans first splashed about in the pleasantly hot natural springs. The temperature still varies between 30°C and 46°C (86°F to 115°F) but today's visitors have the added advantage of a three star hotel in the Calle Baños.

Holidaymakers with no such problems usually head for Aguadulce, Roquetas de Mar or Almerimar on the west side of the Bay of Almería. **Aguadulce** is the oldest, an entirely predictable seaside resort with a couple of perfectly acceptable hotels, a few furnished apartments, discos, night life and facilities for all types of water sports. There are street markets on the 1 and 15 of every month and a fiesta in mid-July but nothing of any historical interest. However this does not really matter because Almería city is only a short bus ride away.

**Roquetas de Mar** has other interests apart from entertaining tourists. It started life as an insignificent little agricultural village on an arid plain with a small fishing port almost attached. Now it is surrounded by orchards and plastic greenhouses and the port is geared to the requirements of fishermen and visitors alike. The village has also spawned a highrise tourist development on the coast about 3km (2 miles) away with wide streets, a good many shops, restaurants and bars as well as discos and other places of entertainment. There are several adequate hotels and plenty of furnished accommodation but no official campsite. It also boasts a yacht club and an 18-hole golf course which is open all year round, except on Mondays, and can supply all the necessary equipment if required. For anyone without a car, buses link Roquetas de Mar with the city, 19km (12 miles) to the north-east. The village and its overgrown

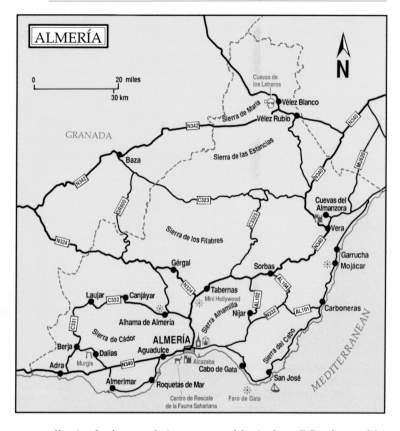

offspring both stage their own annual festivals on 7 October and 26 July respectively.

**Almerimar**, which has virtually all the same attractions but somewhat fewer in each category, takes its golf very seriously, providing enthusiasts with a first class hotel, an excellent 18-hole course and plenty of equipment for hire. With its villas, apartments and marina it is the main coastal resort for El Ejido, the pivot round which the highly lucrative market garden industry revolves.

On the far side of a salt lake, memorable chiefly for its waterfowl, is the somewhat disappointing town of **Adra**. It was originally a Phoenician port of call, then a Roman harbour, and wormed its way into the history books when Boabdil, the last Moorish king of Granada, finally turned his back on Spain and sailed for Africa. The

*The semi-desert area of Almería has often been used for filming Westerns, The film sets are now tourist attractions*

hotels and restaurants are hardly worth mentioning but the handful of first, second and third grade campsites could prove useful for anyone using a tent or towing a caravan and heading for the border with Granada, a few kilometres to the west. The town's sole claim to fame these days is the *El Cortijero Robao*, a dance which is said to have been handed down since the time of the Phoenicians and is seen to good effect during the September festival.

Inland from Adra and about 50km (31 miles) distant, is the elderly village of **Berja**, surrounded by vineyards that have been famous for years. It stands in a valley in the foothills of the Alpujarra mountains not far from **Dalais** which has managed to retain a vestige of the Roman town of *Murgis*. The countryside to the north is somewhat ambiguously described as a recreation area. There are certainly places to picnic, a variety of birds and small animals which provide some modest shooting, plus unpretentious woodlands in the Andarax Valley near the town of Laujar.

**Gérgal**, on the main road from Granada, is another typical small town with a privately-owned and much restored castle which is out of bounds to visitors. The only reason why anyone ever mentions it is that the important Calar Alto observatory is situated close by. The atmospheric conditions are such that astronomers can get a clear view of the stars much more frequently than is possible from other centres in Europe which makes it one of the leading installations of its kind on the Continent. In addition a solar energy research station in the vicinity is investigating the possibilities of generating electricity from the sun and is feeding the results into the national grid.

Roughly at the point where the Granada highway meets the main road from Murcia, near the Rambla de Tabernas, is one of Almería's best known idiosyncrasies, aptly titled **Mini Hollywood**. The surrounding area is bleak and barren but with all the fascination and dramatic impact of the surface of the moon. During the 1960s it was a film maker's paradise. Mini Hollywood is a well preserved relic from those golden days, earning its keep by holding up stage coaches, laying on gun fights and recreating other Wild West diversions for the benefit of its paying customers.

Anyone who finds the atmosphere rather too commercialised can head for the **Decorados Cinematograficas** on the opposite side of the main road. Admittedly this means negotiating an extremely hazardous section, part of which runs along a dry river bed, and climbing up the rock-strewn bank on a track far better suited to a jeep, but the frontier town at the other end looks a good deal more authentic. It is a bit run down, some of the façades need a coat of paint and the Indian wigwams have the air of a desolate village long since abandoned by the tribe, but with a little imagination it could be genuine.

**Tabernas** itself is a very ordinary little place overlooking an oasis of palms and orange trees with nothing of interest apart from an ancient fortress. However, **Níjar**, to the south-east, has been famous for pottery ever since its ruined castle was inhabited. It is full of busy workshops turning out ceramics and with people weaving a distinctive rough cloth which is known as *jarapas*. **Sorbas**, with its white houses balanced precariously along the edge of a cliff beside the road to Murcia, is also well known for its pottery whereas **Macael** is renowned for a particularly beautiful type of white marble. The industry is said to have originated in the thirteenth century and supplied large quantities to the Nasrid kings when they were building the Alhambra in Granada.

There is no direct road linking Macael with **Lijar**, nor, for that matter, is there any particularly good reason for going there. However a most amusing story is told about it. Apparently King Alfonso XII was insulted during a visit to Paris in 1883 and this so incensed the villagers that they promptly declared war on France. No shots were fired but the hostilities lasted for 100 years. In 1983 the French

Consul in Málaga decided that the time had come to put an end to this state of affairs. He drove up to Lijar and signed a formal peace treaty on 3 October.

Tucked away in the north of the province, on the road from Granada to Puerto Lumbreras in Murcia, are the small towns of **Vélez Rubio** and **Vélez Blanco**. Between them are the Cuevas de los Letreros, a prehistoric cavern where the original inhabitants scrawled on the walls in much the same way as their contemporaries were busy doing elsewhere. They did not produce any lifelike pictures to compare with the cave drawings of Altamira and Lascaux but they did leave behind a 5,000-year-old symbol known as the *indalo*. It is an engaging little matchstick figure with outstretched arms supporting a semi-circle over its head.

Vélez Rubio has an eighteenth-century church and a small hostel where it is possible to get a bedroom with a private bath for the night. Vélez Blanco contributes a sixteenth-century castle built by the Marquez del Vélez and a small church which is said to have replaced an early mosque. Both towns hold their own fiestas with Vélez Rubio celebrating in early June and the second week in October while Vélez Blanco prefers the end of May and the second week in August, with religious performances by the Angelus Group between the 24 and 28 December.

Back on the coast a scenic route follows the shoreline, past sand dunes, lonely cliffs and rocky inlets, to the isolated Cabo de Gata lighthouse. Then, skirting a newly-created national park, it swings northwards to **San José**, a small resort with big plans for the future. It already has a pleasure boat harbour and facilities for all types of watersports, especially underwater fishing. Thereafter the road surfaces deteriorate quite considerably but will no doubt improve as more privately owned nudist beaches, some with campsites attached, vie with minute fishing villages for a share of the tourist traffic. Carboneras and Garrucha have already made a very commendable start but they both have a long way to go in order to catch up with Mojácar.

The original village of **Mojácar** is old, distinctly Arab-looking and full of atmosphere. It is piled in a rather haphazard fashion on a hilltop surrounded by plains some 2km (1 mile) from the sea. In comparatively recent times the whole place was in danger of falling into ruins but now many of the houses have been rebuilt and freshly painted hotels have appeared, along with restaurants, souvenir shops and all the apparently essential aids to modern holidaymaking. It is still a pleasure to wander through the narrow, winding streets. The Reyes Católicos *parador* occupies a prime site on

*The town of Mojácar in Almería*

the beach while **Turre**, a few kilometres further inland, has riding stables, tennis courts and a 9-hole golf course. There is a street market every Wednesday, two buses a day to the capital, except on Sundays, and a fiesta on the 28 August in honour of St Augustine.

Two other places of interest within easy reach of Mojácar are **Vera** and **Cuevas del Almanzora**. The former is an attractive old town with some quite worthwhile buildings and the Royal Hospital of St Augustine, founded by the Emperor Charles V in 1521. The latter, not to be outdone, combines the attractions of a medieval castle and Arab fortress with those of some not particularly memorable prehistoric remains at Villaricos. From here a secondary road heads for the coast near San Juan de los Terre, just short of the border with Murcia. Alternatively it is possible to rejoin the main road which calls at Huércal Overa on the way to Puerto Lumbreras.

# 2
# *CÁDIZ*

---

I t has been said, officially, that every village in the province of Cádiz is worth visiting. Although this may be a slight exaggeration certainly most of them are picturesque, some are unusual and just a few could almost be described as unique. The scenery is varied and at times magnificent. There are lonely peaks with a view extending from the highlands of Castilla-La Mancha in the north to the Atlas mountains along the African coast. At slightly lower altitudes the hillsides are coated with oaks, pines and the *pinsapo* (Spanish fir) which has an Alpine look about it but cannot be found anywhere else. Gradually these wooded areas are infiltrated by quince, cherry and almond trees, rolling fields of grain, green pastures, prickly pears, olive groves, vines and oranges. The final contrast is provided by the coastal strip with its marshlands and vast expanses of golden sand washed by Atlantic breakers which, according to the initiated, offer some of the best surfing of any beach in Europe.

Cádiz is the most southerly of all the Andalucían provinces and therefore, naturally, of Spain itself. The Costa de la Luz, which it shares with Huelva, stretches from the Portuguese border to Tarifa, barely 14km (9 miles) from Morocco across the Straits of Gibraltar. Beyond this point the coastline takes a turn to the north-east past the Bay of Algeciras to join Málaga on the Costa del Sol. The province's only other neighbour is Sevilla, lying along its northern border through mountainous country peppered with small white villages, some of them thought to have been frontier posts in the days of the Phoenicians. They have been fought over by the Moors and the Christians, harassed by pirates and used as hideouts by bandits, fugitives and common criminals. These days they take life much more easily, concentrating mainly on local crafts and offering a wide range of attractions.

Surprisingly few tourists in their air-conditioned coaches show much interest in Cádiz, thereby leaving the way clear for travellers to wander round at will. These individual holidaymakers fall into all the predictable categories. Motorists who are determined to cast a hasty eye over as many provincial capitals as possible usually choose the main road or the *autopista* from Sevilla to the city of Cádiz. The former is a marginally better choice for anyone who feels inclined to refresh themselves with a glass of wine in Jerez, which has the added advantage of a direct link with the main route to Arcos de la Frontera. This skirts the Sierra del Pinar to reach Antiquerra, with the option of driving on to Granada or branching off to the right for an easy run to Málaga, the provincial capital on the shores of the Mediterranean. Visitors with slightly more time at their disposal, or who prefer the sea to the mountains, might well opt for the alternative major road to Tarifa. However this tends to ignore the Atlantic seaboard for most of the time although it does put out one or two little feeler roads, most of which end abruptly as soon as they reach an isolated fishing village. No doubt this will completely change as holiday resorts spring up along the beaches with their full quota of highrise buildings, villas, cafés and coloured sun umbrellas. In fact in some places they are already starting to make a tentative appearance. Beyond Tarifa the road heads northwards to Algeciras, bypasses Gibraltar and presses on in a determined fashion to cross the border and lose itself in Málaga's frenetic coastal highway.

A cartwheel of secondary roads, with Medina Sidonia as its central pivot, links all the larger towns and villages scattered throughout the province, from the Gualadquivir delta to the Campo de Gibraltar and from Cape Trafalgar to the northern lakes and hunting areas. However there is no direct road across the western marshes which belong to Huelva and Sevilla, with the river forming the natural boundary. This is an area where time has passed almost unnoticed, leaving little thatched houses that look as if they might have belonged to Bronze Age families and where wild cattle and the odd camel are in danger of extermination from the encroaching rice fields and ambitious reclamation programmes. The area is also a staging post for thousands of migrating birds on their way backwards and forwards between Europe and the African continent, and home to quantities of small game which are now being protected in areas that were once happy hunting grounds for kings and princes. Cádiz also has a network of tiny lanes and cart tracks that amble off with no apparent object in view. These are best ignored by drivers who do not want to find themselves running out of road with no option except to turn round and negotiate all the same potholes again.

For people who feel disinclined to drive all the way down to Southern Spain there is a national airport at Jerez with services to Madrid, Barcelona, Valencia and Palma de Mallorca as well as Tenerife and Las Palmas in the Canary Islands. One of the main railway lines from Madrid calls at Sevilla, with pauses at Jerez and Puerto de Santa María before arriving in the capital, whereas the other crosses the Malága border to end its journey at Algeciras. There are bus and coach services to places of interest such as Arcos de la Frontera, Tarifa, Sanlúcar de Barrameda and others further afield in Andalucía as well as ferries to the Canary Islands, Mallorca, Málaga, Almería and North Africa. Tarifa has a 30 minute hydrofoil trip to Tangier in the summer which only takes fractionally longer than catching the ferry from the capital to Puerto de Santa María on the opposite side of the Bay of Cádiz.

Holiday accommodation is just as easy to come by. Cádiz itself has three comfortable hotels with plenty of small establishments, especially in the vicinity of the Plaza San Juan de Dios. Algeciras heads its list with two four-star hotels followed by many of the less up-market variety but, like any other port, some of these at the lower end of the scale can be decidedly unattractive. Arcos de la Frontera is the only town with a *parador* but several coastal resorts like Conil, Rota and Chipiona have some very acceptable accommodation to offer, although none can hold a candle to the luxury Tenis Hotel in Sotogrande. At least seven different towns have camping sites in the vicinity, including Tarifa where there are no less than four to choose from, although they may well be crowded at the height of the season. The restaurants and bars, especially those along the coast, are famous for the quality and variety of their seafood dishes.

Cádiz province is particularly rich when it comes to fairs and festivals. The capital starts the annual ball rolling with its February Carnival, believed by many people to have its roots in the Isis Feast of Ancient Rome. Whatever the truth of the matter it was banned all over Spain, first by the Inquisition and later by General Franco, although Cádiz ignored the dictator's orders and took to the streets with floats and caricatures, music and fancy dress once a year throughout the whole time he was in office. Carnival is followed by the unquestionably Christian celebrations of Holy Week and Corpus Christi, fairs of various descriptions, exhibitions, concerts, regattas, horse and motor races and mock versions of ancient battles, culminating in a National Flamenco Competition in December.

Historically Cádiz claims to be a great deal older than anywhere else in Western Europe and even has a sneaking feeling that it may have been part of Atlantis before that mythical continent sank to the

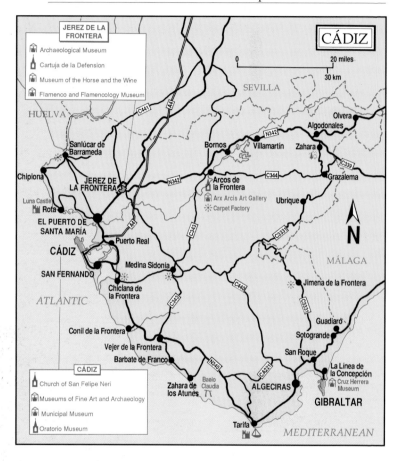

JEREX DE LA FRONTERA
- Archaeological Museum
- Cartuja de la Defension
- Museum of the Horse and the Wine
- Flamenco and Flamencology Museum

CÁDIZ

SEVILLA

HUELVA

Olvera
Algodonales
Sanlúcar de Barrameda
Bornos
Villamartín
Zahara
Chipiona
JEREZ DE LA FRONTERA
Arcos de la Frontera
Grazalema
Luna Castle
Rota
Arx Arcis Art Gallery
Ubrique
Carpet Factory
EL PUERTO DE SANTA MARÍA
Puerto Real
CÁDIZ
MÁLAGA
SAN FERNANDO
Medina Sidonia
ATLANTIC
Chiclana de la Frontera
Jimena de la Frontera
Guadiaro
Conil de la Frontera
Sotogrande
Vejer de la Frontera
San Roque
Barbate de Franco
La Línea de la Concepción
CÁDIZ
Zahara de los Atunes
Baelo Claudia
ALGECIRAS
Cruz Herrera Museum
- Church of San Felipe Neri
- Museums of Fine Art and Archaeology
- Municipal Museum
- Oratorio Museum
GIBRALTAR
Tarifa
MEDITERRANEAN

bottom of the ocean, leaving nothing behind apart from its name.

There were undoubtedly prehistoric communities living in caves in the area many thousands of years ago. If the incredibly wealthy kingdom of *Tartessus* was not exactly centred on the province at least it was not very far away and is believed to have included a settlement overlooking the Bay of Cádiz. The Phoenicians, obeying the instructions of their oracle, built a trading station on the site in 1100BC which they called *Gadir* in honour of Neptune's son who had a large following in the area.

The Carthaginians were not far behind them and even Hannibal looked in for a while before setting out on his famous journey

*The city of Cádiz*

*The Plaza de España, Cádiz*

through Spain and France to Italy. As was only to be expected, this important staging post attracted the attention of the Romans who took it over, changed its name to *Gades* and, with Julius Caesar in control, built it up into a city. The Visigoths made one or two changes of their own, adding a number of new buildings in Vejar and Alcalá, but it was the Moors who made the greatest impact on the province as a whole.

The city of **Cádiz** is one of most delightful of all the Andalucían capitals but unfortunately, even without being unduly critical, the approach to it is enough to put anyone off. The main road, like the railway, swings round in a drunken semi-circle through marshes, salt flats and unprepossessing industrial developments. The *autopista* takes a short cut that is not much better and the two meet up in an exceedingly boring area full of high but undistinguished apartment blocks and lookalike buildings with nothing remotely interesting to encourage the first-time visitor. The only indication that the whole trip has not been a waste of time comes at the Puerta de Tierre, the ancient and pleasantly photogenic entrance to the old city.

The traffic swirls past a large roundabout in the Plaza de la Constitución and under a wide, creeper-covered arch in the solid stone walls, built originally to protect the peninsula. It is just possible to sneak in along one of the two roads on either side of the isthmus but in neither case is the change of atmosphere so obvious. The Puerta de Tierra also has a smaller ornamental gateway leading to a tall, no-nonsense sort of tower with little lookout posts attached to each corner at the top, resembling matching salt and pepper pots. Below is a large pool surrounding a fountain which plays intermittently and two marble columns with statues that appear to be studying the stars.

Beyond the Plaza de la Victoria, on the opposite side of the entrance, a considerable number of straight, narrow streets lined with tall buildings set off purposefully in all directions. It does not really matter which one you choose because the whole conglomeration is surrounded by the sea and the only three routes out are the same as the three roads in. Nevertheless, the easiest and best place to start a sightseeing tour is probably at the eighteenth-century cathedral whose domes and towers completely dwarf the narrow line of buildings that separate them from the water.

This large church is pleasantly ornamental without being over decorative and keeps the majority of its most valuable possessions in the treasury museum. The sculptures by Roldana and Martínez Montañés, like the choir, are worth more than a casual glance and so is the crypt with its tomb of Manuel de Falla. Just round the corner, and even closer to the sea, is the Church of Santa Cruz which was the city's original cathedral.

On the far side of a cluster of small alleys which make up the historic El Populo district, is the Plaza de San Juan de Dios, an attractive square full of palms and open-air cafés. Beyond it, on the far side of the Avenida Ramon de Carranza, is the main port with its full compliment of cargo ships, ferries and pleasure craft. At the other end the avenue blends unobtrusively into the Plaza de España with its large monument in the centre commemorating Las Cortes, the valiant but eventually unproductive attempt at self-determination that began in 1810.

About three blocks away is the Plaza de Mina, a delightful square where the resident Museums of Fine Arts and Archaeology share the same building. The former is justifiably proud of its Zurbarán canvases, most of which were painted during the 10 year period from 1630 to 1640.

The Archaeology Museum makes a feature of its Phoenician exhibits, comprised mainly of sculptures and jewellery, as well as Paleolithic and Neolithic relics and the splendid Anthropoid Siconian Sarcophagus. The Romans are represented by statues and other stone work and there is an interesting but battered pulpit with niches for the figures, one of which is an attractive version of the Virgin and Child. Somewhat incongruously there is also a section devoted to traditional marionettes and the scenery used for their performances.

The Oratorio de Santa Cueva, quite close by, is memorable partly for its Goya frescoes and partly because it inspired Haydn to compose the *Oratory of the Seven Words of the Holy Grotto of Cádiz* after a visit to the city. By way of contrast the Alameda de Apodaca, about the same distance away in the opposite direction, is a kind of parapit edged with balustrades and pairs of tall, decorative light standards. It looks right out over the bay and is especially popular with people who enjoy either watching or painting sunsets. Further on, round the corner, the Parque Genovés, its walkways fringed with palms and cypress trees, makes a perfect setting for the José María Pemán Theatre where open-air productions are staged during the season.

Turning back towards the centre of the old city, past Fragela House with its Byzantine tablets, the Church of San Felipe Neri and the Municipal Museum can be found at opposite ends of the same block. The former is a modest little building, oval inside with a Murillo painting of the Virgin Mary over the altar and a very special place in Spanish history. It was the site chosen for the Free Spanish Parliament which produced its constitution in 1812. The Municipal Museum has an historical theme. Its most prized possession is a scale model of the city as it was at the end of the eighteenth century, made entirely of ivory and mahogany.

Further down the Calle Sacramento the old Tavira watch tower is within a stone's throw of the Plaza Topete, named after a Phoenician temple and now the centre of the market area which is attractively quaint in some respects although it is also entirely functional. Other places worth visiting are the nearby Del Carmen Hospice with a painting by El Greco in the chapel, the Plaza del Tio de la Tiza which revels in its barbecues, and the Playa de la Caleta a sheltered beach below the ancient walls. The Barrio de la Viña is another area worth exploring on account of its narrow streets, whitewashed houses and wrought iron grilles that make excellent trellises for climbing plants and pots. There are traditional taverns and seafood restaurants, stately homes with sculptured doorways and barley sugar pillars, decorative buildings like the Church of San José, modern shops and large open spaces with parking facilities such as the Plaza de San Antonio, presided over by a dignified white church of the same name.

Across the bay from Cádiz is El Puerto de Santa María, an extremely popular seaside resort reached either by the El Vapor ferry from the capital or along the main road to Sevilla. Motorists have a slight advantage because they can stop off at **San Fernando**, on the Isla de Lión, more or less surrounded by salt flats. Until about 100 years ago it was known as Real Puento de Lión, a maritime centre overlooked by the castle of San Romualdo which was built on the orders of Alfonso the Wise to discourage any pirates who might be planning to attack the area. The town proved to be reliable and resourceful, besides putting its Teatro de las Cortes at the disposal of the short-lived Spanish parliament. As a result the name was changed and it was raised to the status of a city. Among its more outstanding features are the Carraca Arsenal, the Pantheon of Illustrious Mariners and an antiquated Carmelite convent.

Slightly further on the road calls in at **Puerto Real**, known to the Romans as *Portus Gaditanus*. It is a self-important little town with a sixteenth-century church and the extensive pine forest of Las Canteras. Both the local campsite and the beach are within reach of El Trocadero which still has the pungent atmosphere of a typical fishing village.

Although **El Puerto de Santa María** is younger by quite a few centuries it is both larger and much better known. The harbour is its most important asset, and has been so ever since it played a minor role in opening up the lucrative trade routes to America about 400 years ago. Nowdays it is more concerned with sherry exports from Jerez and from its own cellars, many of which are open to the public during working hours. The town has its fair share of antiquated buildings including the carefully restored Castle of San Marcos with its walls and towers, the twelfth-century monastery of Nuestra Señora de la Victoria and the Baroque Church of San Francisco.

In a more modern vein, the bullring, which has only been in existence for about 100 years, is one of the most prestigious in Andalucía wheras the low, white, Arab-style casino was added in 1979. So far it is the only one of its kind in the west of the region. For people who prefer to spend their time in the open-air there are the golden sands of Valdelagrana, Vista Hermosa which also has a 9-hole golf course, and Fuentebravia, all overlooked by seaside hotels and private villas and scattered with beach huts. The town lays on a variety of entertainments for its visitors from cock fights, bull fights and pigeon shooting to more universally acceptable spectator sports such as regattas, tennis matches and swimming competitions.

A minor road more or less follows the coastline, passing a campsite at La Mata, until it reaches **Rota** on the northern tip of the Bay of Cádiz. This town is something of an acquired taste with an old section, partly isolated by medieval walls and watched over by the remains of Luna Castle, dating from the thirteenth century. It is somewhat brash and extrovert with a selection of hotels and restaurants and all the entertainments one would expect to find so close to an American naval base.

From here the road, the coastline and the railway keep each other company up to **Chipiona**, an ancient Roman stronghold that has turned itself into a fairly quiet family resort and is certainly none the worse for that. The beaches are just as inviting without being so crowded as those further south and visitors can hear themselves think on the promenade leading to the shrine of Nuestra Señora de la Regla, known for its seventeenth-century cloister beautifully decorated with tiles. Nearby is the ancient lighthouse which has been guiding navigators safely past the mouth of the Guadalquivir for hundreds of years. The town has a comfortable hotel, a sailing club and all the usual holiday facilities.

Although **Sanlúcar de Barrameda** masquerades under the title of a fishing port there is a great deal more to the town. It was the jumping off point for Columbus on his third voyage across the Atlantic and had a visit from Magellan before he headed westwards in an attempt to circumnavigate the globe. The old quarter, clustered round its essentially businesslike Castle of Santiago, is full of attractive little streets and ancient houses, not to mention an odd palace or two, but is more usually visited on account of its wine cellars. The town is the birthplace of *manzanilla* a particularly delectable dry sherry which is said to get its unusual flavour through being in constant contact with the sea air. Nor is it short of more predictable tourist attractions such as the churches of Desamparados and San Nicolás, Trinidad and San Francisco and the convent of Santo Domingo. However, more important than all the rest is the Church of Nuestra Señora de la O on the Plaza de la Paz with its arresting Mudéjar doorway dating from the sixteenth century. The port was an ancient fiefdom of the Dukes of Medina Sidonia and their palace, while fairly nondescript from one angle, has a wide stone frieze that looks as though it might have been inspired by the temples of the Incas.

People with no interest whatsoever in either wine or ancient buildings will also find plenty to do in Sanlúcar de Barrameda. Apart from all the usual water sports, with two clubs on hand to help if necessary, there are long sandy beaches where horse races are held during the season, and various types of game to be seen in the adjacent Algaida Reserve. The town makes a feature of the Appel Fair in May besides being well known for its Corpus Christi celebrations a few weeks later and the summer Festival of the Exaltation of the Guadalquivir.

**Jerez de la Frontera**, an easy drive from the resort, is just as widely known internationally as the capital itself. Although it does not claim to have any connection with Hercules there is a certain amount of evidence to link it to the Moors. The city began life as *Ceret* in Roman times, was renamed *Scherish* by the Arabs, progressed to *Xérès* and finally settled on Jerez. There are no Roman remains to speak of whereas the Alcázar, now little more than a selection of ancient walls surrounded by flowers and shrubs, a twelfth-century octagonal tower and the remnants of the somewhat younger baths, recall the days when it was part of the Emirate of Córdoba.

Following its capture by Alfonso the Wise palaces and churches began to appear with monotonous regularity, fairly widely spaced throughout the original town. Behind the Alcázar is the Collegiate Church of Santa María, beautifully sited and liberally decorated in the early seventeenth century at the top of a wide Baroque stairway. More or less facing the main door a free-standing bell tower comes into its own once a year when crowds gather outside to hear the official proclamation of the current grape harvest. Still more steps, followed by a short walk through some pleasant streets and alleys, lead to the Plaza de la Asunción where the former chapterhouse contains the modest Archaeological Museum. At the opposite end is  the Mudéjar church of San Dionisio, one of several places worth seeing in the surrounding area. Numbered among the palaces are those of the Marqués de Bertemati and the profusely decorated Montana Palace which is now the home of the Marqués de Domecq, a name familiar to sherry lovers the world over.

Armed with an informative map of the city, and a pair of comfortable walking shoes, it is a simple matter to track down the Santo Domingo Convent with its Gothic cloister and the Church of Santiago, dating from the late fifteenth century with a tower that was added 200 years later. Beyond it is the delightful Tempul Park which contains a small zoo.

On the opposite side of the Alcázar and the flower-filled Plaza del Arenal is the church of San Miguel whose retable was created by Martínez Montañés and José de Arce. Some 5km (3 miles) further on, along the road to Medina Sidonia, is the Cartuja de la Defensión. It  is a magnificent fifteenth-century monastery with one of the most memorable façadas in Andalucía and a beautiful cloister surrounded by lofty arches and decorative pillars with nothing to detract from the feeling of spaciousness apart from a fountain in the middle. For a while the monastery was deeply involved in breeding the famous Carthusian horses which retained the name even after they were moved to new quarters in the considerably younger Recreo de las Cadenas Palace.

Horses, like bulls and grapes, are the life blood of Jerez so it is hardly surprising that the Cadenas Palace also finds room for a comprehensive Museum of the Horse and the Wine. In addition  there is a Clock Museum in the Palacio de la Atalaya and a museum of what is rather grandly described as Flamenco and Flamencology in the Calle Quintos. Cockfighting and bullfighting are two local spectator sports although all the displays, cavalcades and colourful events of the Week of the Horse Fair in May are less likely to offend the susceptibilities of some foreign visitors. In addition there are quite frequent matches on the ground belonging to the local polo club and motor racing on the comparatively new circuit that was purpose-built for the Spanish Grand Prix which marks the start of the European season.

It is unlikely that anybody who decides to stop over in Jerez will do so without paying a visit to one of the *bodegas*. Probably the most famous, and certainly the most accessible, are those of González Byass and Pedro Domecq, both within easy walking distance of the Alcázar. The former came into being in 1835 and within 20 years had acquired an English partner — Robert Blake Byass. The Domecqs are

Spanish aristocrats, magnificent horsemen renowned for their ability as *rejoneadors*, who do their bullfighting on horseback, as well as for their stables and their fighting bulls. Visitors are shown round the enormous caverns filled with casks, many of them decorated with coats-of-arms or identified by the signatures of famous international personalities to whom they have been presented. Everyone has an opportunity to sample the various blends and buy a bottle or more to take home with them.

When the time comes to move on the motorist is faced with several possibilities, the most intriguing of which is the so-called 'Route of the White Towns'. However, this is something of a misnomer because the villages in question are scattered fairly widely all over the province and it is impossible to visit each one without doing a lot of backtracking. Nevertheless, with a little judicious planning, it is quite possible to select the ones which have the strongest personal appeal and leave the remainder for a subsequent visit. It is also as well to bear in mind that, although these mountain strongholds are seldom very far apart, the roads connecting them are anything but straightforward, and are not always in very good condition, so the only way to enjoy the drive is to allow plenty of time for it.

**Arcos de la Frontera**, the nearest 'white town' to Jerez and only about 40km (25 miles) away, is without doubt the most spectacular of them all. According to legend it was founded by one of Noah's grandsons and, in fact, it would have been quite possible for the Ark to put him ashore at the top of the perpendicular cliff overlooking the Río Guadalete before continuing its voyage across the floodwaters to the Middle East. The approach road climbs up through a comparatively modern suburb, squeezes its way into an opening and immediately is transformed into a tangle of incredibly narrow streets with sharp right-angle turnings.

Fortunately the Plaza de España is close at hand with a limited amount of parking space in the square and a superb view over vineyards, olive groves, orchards and orange trees to the distant line of encircling hills. On the left hand side is the *parador* Casa del Corregidor, a long white building with grilles over the windows and small individual balconies.

Opposite the *parador* is the town hall and behind it a well-preserved Moorish castle, once the property of the Dukes of Arcos, which has given rise to several highly improbable myths and fairy tales. Finally the stalwart, if slightly dilapidated, Church of Santa María de la Anunción completes the picture with an odd statue or two and an extremely solid bell tower that is worth climbing, especially at sunset, in order to admire the view.

*The view from the* parador *at Arcos de la Frontera*

*Arcos de la Frontera; the Church of Santa María de la Anunción*

Nearby, along the imaginatively named Alley of the Clock Weights, the seventeenth-century Convent of the Encarnación with its carved doorway is a prelude to several elderly buildings, among them the Mercedarias Descalzas Convent, looking out rather blindly on to Paradise Street. Its nearest neighbours are the Arx Arcis Art Gallery and a carpet factory which is not averse to casual visitors.

Further along this narrow, rocky spur the ruins of an ancient market share the Calle Núñez de Prado with the Gothic Chapel of the Misericordia and the antiquated El Mayorazgo palace which has been converted into the municipal art school. It is almost in the shadow of the large and lofty Church of San Pedro, thought to have been built on the site of an ancient Arab fortress. San Pedro has its own collection of treasures including a sixteenth-century Madonna and a painting of the Divine Shepherd.

The streets all round are full of atmospheric old houses, some of them sporting window boxes filled with flowers, unexpected little patios and squares and an occasional bar or café tucked away out of sight. It is quite easy to lose one's sense of direction in some of the dark, oriental alleyways, but not for long. They either peter out altogether or else end abruptly on the edge of the steep ravines that surround the greater part of the old town. Arcos is famous for its Holy Week celebrations which include Christ's blessing on the people and the fields at dawn on Good Friday, processions with floats specially designed so that they can be edged through the inadequate space between the buildings, and bullrunning on Easter Sunday.

The town of **Bornos**, 11km (7 miles) away on the main road to Antequera, has a large lake almost to itself but apparently no immediate plans to turn into a holiday playground. However most of the necessary ingredients are there — a dilapidated palace, a fairly typical church, an elderly monastery and just a hint of Roman ruins at Carixa, 5km (3 miles) from the town. The scenery is also very pleasant, consisting largely of wheat and cotton fields, patches of woodland and views across the valley to other villages which all look very much the same. **Villamartín**, for instance, could easily be taken for an Arab town although it only dates back to 1503 when the local inhabitants banded together to lease a piece of land from Sevilla to build a hamlet of their own. They made the streets a trifle wider than usual, got hold of some sculptures for the Church of Las Virtudes and planted hybiscus and bougainvillae.

**Algodonales**, about 25km ($15^1/_2$ miles) further up the road, has an attractive paved walkway, flanked by orange trees, leading to the ornamental doorway of its local parish church but nothing else of interest beyond the fact that it marks the parting of the ways. Motorists in a hurry can continue along the main road as it climbs steadily through open country scented with thyme and rosemary to Puerto de Cabañas. Almost at once it bypasses Torre-Alháquime with the remains of its ancient ramparts and nods at the Baroque Sanctuary de los Remedios. This is within sight of **Olvera**, the last 'white town' of any consequence before the border, sprawling across the hillside like an isolated patch of heavy snow. It is very easy to identify because the small, uniform houses with their slanting red tiled roofs are completely dominated by an outsize nineteenth-century church and the ruins of a medieval fortress growing out of its own solid expanse of rock. It is a pleasing town with all the usual Arab overtones, an unexpectedly straight main street and a reputation for producing saddles, harnesses and other similar leather articles.

A very minor road links Olvera with both Torre-Alháquime and Setenil, one of the last Moorish outposts to be captured by the forces of Castile. The ruined castle held out for about 8 years after the capitulation of Granada and, even today, some of the houses are still cut back into the rock face which helped to protect the defenders.

An alternative and attractively scenic road from Algodonales heads south-eastwards to cross the border into Málaga and makes its way to Ronda. Almost at once there is a turning off to **Zahara**, a good road linked to the village by a bone-shaking, pothole-ridden byway. However it is worth pressing on slowly and carefully to the collection of typical little houses, huddled at the foot of a crag improbably topped by the remains of an ancient fort. The Torre del Reloj and the  Church of Santa María de Mesa are Zahara's main attractions apart from some excellent views and the almost overpowering scent of  orange blossom in the spring. Most of the local pilgrimages take place in June, with some additional celebrations in August, but the most unusual is the anniversary of the Sarracen Liberation on 28 October. The banner which is its centrepiece is said to be the same one that was flown over the fortress on the day it was liberated by the Christians.

Back at the point of entry the well-maintained surface comes as a relief as the road carries on through the mountains to join the main route from Arcos de la Frontera just short of **Grazalema**. Like other villages of its ilk the whole place is a jumbled mass of almost-white houses, hiding behind grille-protected windows and often festooned with flowering plants. Two quite presentable roadways snake their way through from one end to the other, linked by small, silent and almost deserted alleys. The village has been in the blanket

*Zahara with its ancient fortress*

and poncho making business since its early days. They are still made on large looms, which need two people to operate them, and are among the most useful souvenirs to be found in the province.

**Ubrique**, about 20km (12 miles) to the south, insists that it can trace its history back to the Phoenicians although its oldest visible attraction is the fifteenth-century church of Nuestra Señora de la O. In fact the main reasons for including it in any itinerary are to see the scenery and, perhaps, to pick up some leather goods. At one time the local craftsmen were famous for such things as *zurrones* — bags dyed with saffron that were used by hunters — but they now concentrate on supplying the sort of goods demanded by shops all over the country. Beyond Ubrique the same road winds its way through the Sierra del Aljibe to **Alcalá de los Gazules**, a typically sleepy hillside town with so little interest in tradition that it has turned its bullring into a disco. However it is also known for the sparse remnants of the Roman town of *Lascuta* and the much more recent Church of San Jorge.

From here onwards the landscape levels out into meadows and pastures without very much in the way of small hamlets or isolated communities. It is essentially ranching country devoted to the breeding of thoroughbred horses and fighting bulls. The animals wander at will across the grasslands, speckled here and there with olive groves, and are watched over by mounted herdsmen, all of whom carry long staffs that are an essential part of their job. In the spring selected calves and young bulls are separated from the herd and taken to the *tienta*, or testing ring, where they are assessed for their various qualities.

**Medina Sidonia**, the main town in the area, was a frontier post in the fifteenth century when a new line in dukes was created to defend the whole area down to the Bay of Cádiz. The Church of Santa María la Coronada dates back to the late fifteenth century when it was built on the foundations of an earlier castle. Other local attractions include the churches of Santiago and San Agustin, the ducal palace, the eighteenth-century town hall and some antiquated mansions. Among the few bits and pieces left over from the ramparts is the Puerta de la Pastora, a fortified gateway at the top of a much younger flight of shallow steps. There are some mildly interesting caves in the vicinity and the annual Carnival rates a favourable mention in the official tourist brochures.

A fairly uninspiring secondary road links Medina Sidonia with **Chiclana de la Frontera** on the main coastal route from Cádiz to Algeciras. It is a smallish town surrounded by pines and salt flats which has something to offer nearly everyone. The most comfortable hotel is a favourite haunt of people who are convinced that the mineral springs of the Fuente Amarga do wonders for their health, whereas amateur archaeologists head straight for what is left of the Temple of Hercules on the off-shore island of Sancti-Petri. Not that there is much to see because its place has been taken by a lighthouse but at least it has legendary associations with Hannibal, a battered thirteenth century castle and a pleasing beach.

In the meanwhile the town of Chiclana de la Frontera provides some acceptable alternatives such as the Church of San Juan Bautista, the hermitage of Santa Ana and a church belonging to the Augustine monks. After a lazy day on the Barrosa beach, some 9km (6 miles), away it makes a pleasant change to wander through the narrow streets inspecting a selection of typical mansions, calling in on the way at a likely-looking bar for a glass of one of the local white wines known as *pastos*. The town is famous for its traditional dolls which make acceptable presents for the younger members of the family and are often bought simply as souvenirs.

The Campo de San Andres golf course is shared more or less equally between Chiclana and **Conil de la Frontera**, further along the coast. This rapidly expanding town at the mouth of the Río Salado makes no bones about the fact that it is a fishing village which would far rather be a popular holiday resort. New buildings are appearing everywhere, especially along the seafront with its wide sandy beaches that stretch for more than 15km (9 miles). Adequate accommodation is provided by one comfortable hotel and a number of more run-of-the-mill establishments in addition to a campsite. At the moment there are not many organised entertainments and holidaymakers spend their time bathing, windsurfing, fishing, inspecting the ruins of an elderly castle or going for long walks across the dunes.

For motorists in need of a complete change of scenery the hill town of **Vejer de la Frontera** is only just down the road. It is one of the prettiest of all the old Moorish settlements with its flat roofs, steep winding alleys and the crumpled remains of an Alcázar. The original Jewish quarter beside the ramparts has been particularly well preserved and so have some of the medieval houses surrounding the Church of El Salvador. It was built in the thirteenth century on the site of an old mosque but was up-dated several times afterwards which accounts for all the various changes in style. The only thing worth seeing inside is the altarpiece with its many statues and tiles.

The Paseo de las Cobijadas takes its name from the women of the village who used to cover themselves from head to foot in a dark cloak, or *cobija*, which originated either in Africa or the Middle East. Just occasionally one of these *cobijadas* may be seen walking slowly through the older parts of the town. It is a town that is well worth exploring on foot in order to absorb the atmosphere, catch a glimpse of the storks that make their homes there and admire the view across the valley of the Río Barbate and down to the lighthouse at Cape Trafalgar. Foremost among the local celebrations are the events marking Holy Week which end on Easter Sunday with the Toro Embolao, when bulls with cut or padded horns are let loose in the streets.

**Barbate de Franco** could almost be described as Vejer de la Fronterás alloted seaside resort. It is a busy fishing harbour at the mouth of the river with a market where everything not destined for the canning factory is auctioned off. The beaches are predictably inviting, with a number of natural grottos, freshwater springs and plenty of space for all the holidaymakers who crowd on to the sands to take part in the August Sardine Fair. Further along the coast, on the far side of the river, **Zahara de los Atunes** has more weighty matters on its mind. It is one of the main tuna fishing centres which work flat out from April to August, using 2,000 year old methods to bring in the season's catch. Once the fish have been herded into special nets and pulled on board they are transferred to factory ships or taken to the processing plants on shore. Zahara is almost the last place on the road because this has been extended through the dunes to **Atlanterra**. So far it is a splendidly isolated spot with a few up-market villas, comfortable accommodation and almost deserted beaches stretching down to the very limits of the Costa de la Luz.

**Tarifa**, on the southernmost tip of Spain, is an exceedingly old town which was the starting point for the Moorish invasion nearly 1,300 years ago. It was named after Tarif Ben Malik whose enthusiasm persuaded Count Julian of Ceuta to pit his strength against the Visigoths. The invasion was so successful that within 3 years the Arab armies had crossed the Pyrénées and were pressing on into France. For more than five centuries the local Moors remained in control but in 1292 their fortress at Tarifa was overrun by the Christians led by Alonso Pérez de Guzmán. The Moors counter-attacked, threatening to kill his son whom they had taken hostage. Guzmán's scornful gesture of defiance saved the castle and made him a national hero.

The original fortress with its octagonal tower and obviously effective ramparts is still used as a barracks, but there are guided tours twice a week for those who want to picture the scene from the commander's standpoint on the battlements with views of the Rif Mountains in North Africa. Tarifa is a delightful little place with a few other Moorish remains, the churches of Santa María and San Pedro, atmospheric cobbled streets and some of the best beaches to be found anywhere, all facing the coast of Africa. Although the town is not particularly tourist orientated it has a handful of acceptable hotels, at least two with tennis courts and swimming pools, a choice of campsites, various sports facilities including a windsurfing club with possibly the finest windsurfing to be found anywhere in Europe, and a hydrofoil service to Tangier in the summer.

Bolonia Beach, between Punta Paloma and Cape Camarinal, has an additional attraction in the form of the Ancient Roman town of **Baelo Claudia**. Parts of it have already been excavated and it is possible to walk along the main street, still bearing the marks of heavy traffic after nearly 2,000 years, climb up the steps to the Temple of Jupiter and make out the site of the theatre and the marketplace. There is still a lot of work to be done, especially when it comes to uncovering the remains of the villas which may hold several items of interest such as mosaic floors in the various rooms and courtyards.

From Tarifa the highway takes leave of the coast and makes for **Algeciras**, a town which has probably had the worst press notices of any place in Spain. Certainly it requires a conscious effort to find

*The battlements of Tarifa*

*Orchards of oranges and lemons are a familiar sight in Southern Spain*

anything in the way of tourist attractions under the heavy veneer which is common to all busy ports. There are some moderately viewable churches and a few archaeological remains, at least four comfortable hotels, some with excellent sports facilities, a couple of campsites, a sailing club and regular ferry services to Tangier, Ceuta and the Canary Islands. From its vantage point on the Bay of

Algeciras the town has an uninterrupted view of both Gibraltar and the mountains of Morocco on the opposite side of the straits.

Algeciras is also in more or less direct contact with **Jimena de la Frontera**, another of the famous 'white towns' of Cádiz. The scenery on the way up is pleasant without being spectacular, consisting of fairly low hills and wooded valleys filled mainly with cork oak trees. The area was fought over regularly by the Christians and the Moors who managed to hold out in Jimena de la Frontera rather longer than they did in most other hill villages. Their ancient castle, conscientiously restored by its new owners in the late fifteenth century, has been very well preserved and so has the Franciscan convent that was founded at roughly the same time. Other places of interest are the Baroque church of La Coronada and the Church of the Misericorda, although there is nothing very remarkable inside. Just worth mentioning in passing is the nearby hamlet of **Castellar de la Frontera** overlooking the Guadarranque reservoir. The whole place has been rather spoiled by well-meaning attempts to turn it into a holiday centre. All that happened was that the local people exchanged their old homes for new ones when they came on the market, leaving the medieval quarter behind its thirteenth century ramparts to the tender mercies of somewhat irresponsible communes who opened small workshops in an effort to make a living.

Neither **La Línea de la Concepción**, on the border with Gibraltar, nor its neighbour **San Roque** could be fairly described as tourist resorts. However the former has a perfectly acceptable hotel and some unusual paintings in the Cruz Herrera Museum, while the latter runs to an equally acceptable restaurant in the Plaza de Armas and a useful campsite further up the road. Provided money is no object the Tenis Hotel at Sotogrande del Guadiara is undoubtedly the best place to stop. However it is also the most highly-rated hotel in Cádiz province so anyone who is forced to watch the *pesetas* should definitely give it a miss. The options are simple, with a choice of either driving back to Los Barrios or La Linea or pressing on across the border into Málaga.

# 3
# *CÓRDOBA*

Mention Córdoba and most people immediately think of the mosque. Although it is without any doubt the foremost tourist attraction this famous landmark is a very long way from being the only thing the city and the province have to offer. The whole area is steeped in history, patterned with vineyards and olive groves, rich in legends, studded with picturesque villages and often festooned with flowers. Its craftsmen have centuries of tradition behind them, the museums are filled with art and archaeology, the festivals with music and the countryside with game parks and hunting reserves.

Geographically Córdoba is one of the two most northerly provinces of Andalucía. It is bordered by Extremadura and Ciudad Real and enclosed to the west, south and east by Sevilla, Málaga, Granada and Jaén. The Valle de los Pedroches, in the far north, is a land of oaks and granite that merges into the Sierra Morena which it shares with Sevilla and Jaén. The Arabs called it the Plain of Acorns but since that time it has developed a number of additional characteristics such as cattle, pig and sheep farming, barley fields, tree plantations and areas set aside for the preservation of wildlife. Next comes the fertile valley of the Guadalquivir cutting the province more or less in half, edged with vineyards, cereals and interminable olive trees on the Campiña plains. In the deep south-east the Baetic mountain range, spotted with little villages, climbs up towards the Sierra Nevada.

More than a third of the population of Córdoba live and work in the provincial capital, leaving the remainder to concentrate on agriculture, livestock and a certain amount of mining. The outlying towns and villages are quite widely spaced with the majority located towards the south. Many are both eye-catching and historic, clustered round an ancient fortress or an antiquated church, while others are rather more businesslike, functional and, for the moment, supremely indifferent to visitors and to the possible advantages of a growing tourist trade.

The city of **Córdoba** is well placed when it comes to roads and railways but relies largely on Sevilla and Málaga as far as airports are concerned. However the small national airport a few kilometres away has daily services to Madrid and weekly flights to Barcelona and Palma de Mallorca. The main Madrid-Cádiz railway and a branch line to Málaga ensure that there are plenty of trains in each direction, augmented by coaches to Granada and other provincial capitals as well as towns and villages throughout the region itself. Cars are available for hire, there are local buses and some taxis operate round-the-clock, although the little horse-drawn carriages are more fun when it comes to sight-seeing tours in the old quarter of the city. The province is well provided with highways that pass through on their way from Badajoz to Granada and from Sevilla to Madrid with additional major roads to Jaén through Porcuna or Alcalá la Real. A variety of secondary routes take care of most of the larger towns with minor roads and byways offering shortcuts through the mountains for drivers who do not mind if the surfaces deteriorate sometimes.

The origins of Córdoba are almost lost in antiquity. It was certainly an Iberian settlement, although apparently one of no great importance before the Romans first arrived in about 206BC. More than 50 years passed before the city was founded and on its way to becoming a Patrician colony and capital of the Roman province of *Baetica*. Julius Caesar and Pompey settled their differences in the surrounding area, to Caesar's complete advantage. The Visigoths were the next on the scene when King Leovigildus captured the area towards the end of the sixth century, after which nothing much happened until the Moorish invasion of 711.

Córdoba soon emerged under the Arabs as a city of unparalleled influence and importance, a centre of great learning and of incredible magnificence. It had the first street lighting to be installed in Europe, fountains ran with quicksilver and the streets were crowded with foreign intellectuals who could hardly wait to get home to sing its praises. People of all colours and creeds lived peacefully together in what was described at the time as 'the ornament of the world' while literature, music and craftsmanship flourished.

Since the Great Mosque (La Mezquita), is obviously a favourite point of interest with tourists it is an ideal place to start a tour of the city. The building stands on the site of a pagan temple, succeeded by a church after the introduction of Christianity, which in turn was replaced on the orders of Abd-ar-Rahman I during the eighth cen-

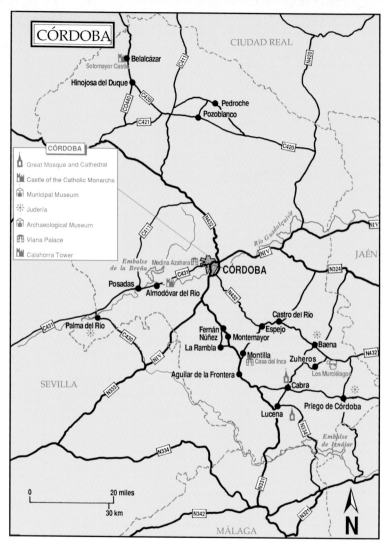

tury. The original construction was enlarged at intervals — a very simple matter where mosques are concerned because they are made up of row upon row of arches supported by sturdy columns so it is only a question of adding additional lines. At present there are literally hundreds of these marble columns, some of which are slightly different from the others because it was common practice to

The ancient bridge at
Córdoba over the Río
Guadalquivir with the
Great Mosque in the
background

Córdoba: Calle
Cardenal Gonzáles

make use of anything suitable that could be scrounged from existing temples, churches and old ruins.

The entrance to the mosque is through a Mudéjar gateway known as the Door of Forgiveness, and across the Court of Orange Trees. Opposite the adjacent belltower that replaced a minaret, the Door of Palms opens into a seemingly endless forest of pillars with their red and white Arab arches receding into the dim distance.

It was El Hakam II, towards the end of the tenth century, who added the Mihrab, a splendidly ornate octagonal chamber embellished with rich mosaics, and a special enclosure reserved for the caliph. The nearby Villaviciosa Chapel and the Chapel Royal were Christian additions that blended in well with their surroundings whereas the cathedral is a self-indulgent mixture of half a dozen different styles all jostled together in an effort to out-do the Moors. There are some beautiful stalls and two highly ornamental pulpits, not to mention a heavenly choir of cherubim, but the contrast be–tween concentrated splendour and sheer simplicity is not to everybody's taste. Many of the cathedral's precious possessions are kept in the treasury, including an enormous monstrance, chalices, shrines and crucifixes, one carved by Alonso Cano. They can be seen by producing the admission ticket which is bought at the Door of Palms.

Facing the west wall of the Great Mosque is the Episcopal Palace, built originally by the Visigoths and adapted by the caliphs as their Alcázar before it was up-dated in the fifteenth and sixteenth centuries. At one end is the Church of San Jacinto with its Gothic doorway and at the other a soaring triumphal monument to the Archangel San Raphael.

The Castle of the Catholic Monarchs, built by Alfonso XI in 1327, also overlooks the river. Foremost among its many attractions are the Hall of Mosaics and what are endearingly described by one guide as 'suggestive' gardens. These are Moorish in style with terraces, ornamental pools, statues, cypress trees and flowerbeds as well as a vegetable patch, said to have been supplying fresh produce since the days of the Visigoths. One of the castle's prize possessions is a superbly carved Roman sarcophagus.

Also in the vicinity of the mosque is the somewhat dilapidated Gate of the Bridge, guarding the city end of the old Roman bridge over the Gaudalquivir. This is really only Roman to the extent that some of the foundations are presumed to be original, the rest has been repaired, reinforced and restored so often that it would be extremely difficult to put a date to it. However no such problem exists in the case of the Calahorra Tower on the opposite bank. It is aggressively medieval and unadorned, surrounded by low stone walls and providing house room for a small museum. This traces the history of Al-Andalus with the help of exceedingly graphic illustrations and also has space for philosophy, music and some armour which belonged to Gonzalo Fernández de Córdoba, better remembered as El Gran Capitán.

At the northern end of the Great Mosque, on the side facing away from the river, is the enchanting Calle de las Flores, best known of all the little flower-filled alleys with their white-washed houses, window grilles and cool, secluded patios. It is far removed in character from the road immediately surrounding the mosque where predictable souvenirs, ranging from ceramics to flamenco-style dresses, are arranged along the pavements as soon as the shops open.

An early start might well be made in Judería, the old Jewish quarter a block or two away, which has recently become quite fashionable. The original entrance through the ramparts was by way of the Almodóvar Gate, not far from the ancient synagogue, one of the only two still to be found in Spain. The square room with its balcony set aside for women has been occupying a site close to the Calle Maimonides for more than 600 years and although it keeps semi-official hours the caretaker will show visitors round almost any morning or late afternoon.

The Municipal Museum, practically next door, is a 'must' for anyone who is interested in bullfighting. It is housed in the Casa de las Bulas and contains a treasure trove of memorabilia recalling in particular the handful of men who were born in the city and made their names, and sometimes their fortunes, in the ring.

Anyone who has no interest in bullfighting would probably prefer to spend the time in other sections of the museum devoted to silver and to traditional leatherwork, both of which have outstanding examples of Córdoba's two most ancient crafts. Apart from the church of San Bartolomé the only other attraction in the vicinity — if you discount the little alleyways with their half arches, cobbles and ivy-covered walls — is the rather odd-looking Casa del Indiano on the Calle Ruano Torres.

A short, brisk walk to the north, past the Casa del Hoces, now the School of Applied Arts and Crafts, and the adjacent one-time home of the Military Government, there are two marginally interesting churches — those of San Nicolás de la Ville with its Renaissance façade and matching tower, and San Hipólito which is slightly larger. Alternatively the churches of La Campania and Santa Victoria, believed to have been inspired by the Pantheon in Rome, keep each other company to the south of the Plaza de las Tendillas — the centre of both the modern town and of the Roman city before it was

*Exterior doorway into the Great Mosque, Córdoba*

down-graded by the Visigoths and the Moors. The square has its full quota of modern shops and crowded cafés but not a great many places to park the car. It is only a stone's throw from the Conservatory of Music and Elocution, which probably accounts for the number of students, and only slightly further removed from the Archaeological Museum.

This national museum,  housed in the Renaissance Palace of Páez, is the largest in Andalucía and certainly among the most absorbing. It delves back into prehistory with Iberian exhibits, passes on to Roman mosaics and items left by the Visigoths, highlights a magnificent collection of Moorish art from the 'Golden Days' of the city as well as Renaissance relics and Baroque.

Heading back towards the river, past the Portillo Arch that was originally a fortified entrance through the ramparts, there is an elderly palace, the Church of San Francisco and the captivating Plaza del Potro which takes its name from the famous sixteenth-century Colt Fountain, topped by a small, prancing horse. Overlooking the

*Córdoba: the Moorish arches and pillars of the Great Mosque*

Córdoba: the interior
of the cathedral

The monument to
Manolete, Spain's
greatest bullfighter,
which receives more
visitors than any other
place in Córdoba

square is the Posada del Potro, an inn immortalised by Cervantes in *Don Quixote* and now much restored and used for displays of leather goods and silver.

The old Hospital of Charity on the opposite side of the plaza has two museums for the price of one. The Fine Arts Museum combines the work of artists of the calibre of Murillo, Goya and Zurbarán, plus an occasional foreign contributor such as Rubens and Titian, with paintings and drawings that trace the development of the Cordovan School. The adjoining Julio Romero de Torres Museum is unlikely to appeal to everyone although it is said to be extremely popular with about fifty paintings by this local exponent of Modernism and Symbolism and was presented by his family after his death in 1930.

Another of Córdoba's memorable squares is the Plaza de la Corredera, built in the seventeenth century, surrounded by arcades and overlooked by dozens of windows which came in very useful in the days when it was used for bullfighting. Cristo de los Faroles, with its rather drunken-looking lanterns, shares the more distant Capuchinos Square with an understated white church and convent of the same name. They are both within easy walking distance of the Manolete Monument and the Viana Palace, once the home of the Marqués del Viana. This is now public property and worth seeing for its many patios, flower-filled garden and elegantly decorated rooms full of pictures, tapestries, antique furniture, porcelain, embossed leather and other objects d'art.

Apart from a handful of additional churches, rather too numerous to mention individually but generally worth inspecting if time is no object, there are several other attractions. These include the Malmuerta Tower, some well preserved mansions, the Royal Stables famous for their horses and the remains of a selection of Arab mills on the banks of the Gualdalquivir. The city hall has recently discovered some Roman ruins on the doorstep whereas the Parque José Cruz Conde turns its back on architecture in favour of a zoo.

With all there is to see it stands to reason that Córdoba makes ample provision for its visitors. There is an occasional first class hotel, one in the Jardines de la Victoria adjoining the ancient city and another, the Parador Nacional La Arruzafa, some three or four kilometres away. It is a modern building, standing in its own gardens full of oleanders and orange trees with tennis, a landscaped swimming pool and everything necessary to ensure the comfort of its guests. A handful of less up-market establishments are grouped round the mosque in addition to which a number of smaller hotels and hostels are dotted all about the city. With well over fifty different restaurants to choose from it is simply a question of deciding whether to sample traditional Andalucían dishes, stick to an international menu or eat in the Chinese or Italian style.

Anyone who feels like a change from sightseeing can opt for a riding club, the 18-hole golf course of Los Villares, football match, bull fight, some modest car racing or join in the ever-popular hunt for souvenirs. The city's Municipal Orchestra gives Sunday concerts in the Alcázar, an International Guitar Festival is held during the summer but the National Flamenco Contest only takes place at 3-yearly intervals, replaced at other times by a great many less rarified performances, particularly in the Zoco near the old synagogue.

The annual calendar of events begins with Carnival followed by the impressive Holy Week processions when spectators can reserve a seat along the route, thoughtfully provided by the Association of Brotherhoods. A Contest of Popular Patios marks the Crosses of May festivities in the early part of the month when every square is more than usually festooned with flowers and filled with music and dancing, interrupted only by a Sunday pilgrimage to the Sanctuary of Linares. The Feria de Nuestra Señora de la Salud is a very dressy affair at the end of May.

Some 10km (6 miles) west of Córdoba excavation work is going on at the site of **Medina Azahara**, described variously as the Arabian Nights Palace or the Cordovan Versailles. Building began in 936 on this City of Flowers to provide a country residence for Abd-ar-Rahman III but one thing led to another, each more costly than the last. Eventually it extended over three terraces on the slopes of the Sierra Morena with gardens separating the mosque from the Alcázar at the top. The Berbers razed it to the ground in 1013 but in the early 1940s Medina Azahara was rediscovered and plans were drawn up to restore at least part of the ruins. So far it is possible to visit the salons of the caliphs and their viziers, look round the mosque, walk through the gardens and inspect all the items uncovered by archaeologists housed in a small museum on the site.

Córdoba province north of the Guadalquivir is rather more suited to the outdoor enthusiast than the confirmed sightseer. There are one or two reservoirs, a couple of campsites within reach of the river, a sprinkling of mines and a good many ranches but few towns of any real consequence. Down stream on the road to Posadas, the well preserved castle of **Almodóvar del Río** claims to be one of the best examples of a hilltop fortress in Andalucía — an extravagant boast in view of all the strong competition, although it certainly does look most impressive.

The **Embalse de la Breña**, quite close by, is making a determined effort to find its feet as a popular holiday playground and already provides facilities for all kinds of water sports and is the home of the somewhat unexpected Yacht Club of Córdoba. It also provides fishermen with a choice of black bass or carp.

The main road from Córdoba city to Badajoz, in Extremadura, follows the railway up to Espiel without finding anything particularly attractive along the way. From here a secondary route branches off northwards to join the C420 near Alcaracejos which guards the entrance to the valley and has something to offer on either hand.

Turn to the west and the first place of interest is **Hinojosa del Duque** with a disproportionately large fifteenth century church dedicated to St John the Baptist and known respectfully, if inaccurately, as the 'Cathedral of the Sierra'. Slightly further on, and surrounded by cornfields, the oddly shaped Homage Tower of Sotomayor Castle keeps an ancient eye on the village of **Belalcázar**, founded during the Moorish occupation when it was known as *Gafig*. The village is so close to Extremadura that one of its more adventurous sons, Sebastián de Belalcázar, joined forces with the Conquistador Francisco Pizarro, who lived in Trujillo, and went off with him to conquer Peru. The outlying Convento de la Columna only admits visitors who have made an appointment beforehand but inspite of this it is well known for its home-made cakes.

**Pozoblanco**, the modern capital of the region, lies to the east of Alcaracejos and is a fairly run-of-the-mill sort of town with a brace of churches and two essentially forgettable hotels. However it has both a bullring and a golf course — so far one of the very few in Córdoba — and introduces an historical note with the tomb of Juan Gines de Sepulveda in the Church of Santa Catalina. It took over its leading role from **Pedroche**, the original Capital of the Seven Villages, whose castle was destroyed by the Catholic Monarchs, although part of it went towards building the tall church tower. Spring is a good time to visit the area when everyone is in festive mood.

There is unquestionably more variety to the south of the Guadalquivir. **Palma del Río**, almost on the border with Sevilla, combines orange trees with ancient ramparts and throws in two elderly churches for good measure. However it is the wine route that attracts the most visitors. A choice of two major routes head south from the capital, linked at intervals by secondary roads and a good many minor ones, so it is possible to plan an outing to fit in with the time available.

In the first instance, the road to Málaga slices its way through vineyards to **Montilla** where the Alvear *bodega* is not only the largest in the region but also claims to be the oldest in Spain. It came into being in 1729 producing wine so like the famous sherry of Jerez that

*Córdoba: the Calahorra Tower*

the name of the town was borrowed and incorporated as *amontillado*. Near the old market place is the Casa del Inca, once the home of the sixteenth-century writer Garcilaso de la Vega who devoted all his attention to the history of the Inca empire. Now, appropriately, it is used partly to house the local library. Nearby are several other antiquated houses, convents and churches including La Encarnación which, for some reason, was chosen as the final resting place of San Juan de Avila. One of the only three-star hotels in Córdoba, apart from those in the capital, can be found in Montilla, along with some smaller hostels, restaurants and little bars where the local wine flows freely.

This so-called 'Capital of the Vineyards' is a good base from which to explore a number of small, atmospheric towns in the vicinity. Fernán Núñez and Montemayor have a ducal palace apiece while La Rambla is the place to go in search of pottery. Aguilar de la Frontera, founded by the Greeks, possesses an eye-catching clock-tower, three pleasing little churches and the attractive, octagonal San José Plaza, whereas Monturque further down the road, can produce enough evidence to show that it was once a Roman settlement. They are all relatively quiet and relaxed, when compared with Lucena.

Although twentieth-century **Lucena** can hardly be described as an important centre it is certainly a busy one. The local factories and cottage industries turn out a variety of articles, mainly in copper, brass and bronze, which, in addition to a successful line in oil lamps, are sold throughout the country and exported overseas.

Apart from one or two adequate hotels and hostels and some small potteries the town has a handful of historic attractions, the majority of which are churches. The most memorable of these is San Mateo because of the Sacrarium Chapel, generally believed to be the work of José Churriguera whose much admired tendency to over decorate was taken to extraordinary lengths after his death in 1725. The Moral Tower is considerably older and more famous because Boabdil, the last Moorish ruler of Granada, was imprisoned there for a while after an ill-advised attack on the local Christians in 1483. The town is known for its Holy Week processions, May Festivals and celebrations connected with the grape harvest in September.

South of Lucena, the small town of **Rute** would probably never get an honourable mention in any tourist brochure for its two parish churches but it has another, quite different, attraction. It has spawned something like fifteen or sixteen different distilleries all actively engaged in making *anis*. This is an extremely potent drink derived from anise seeds.

From Rute it is only a few kilometres to the Embalse de Iznájar, a pleasing reservoir stocked with trout and presided over by a village of the same name. On the other hand two small mountain roads finger their way across country to **Priego de Córdoba**, considered by some people to be one of the loveliest hill towns in Andalucía. It has grown up over the centuries in a narrow river valley at the foot of the highest mountain peak in the province and receives comparatively few visitors considering that it is just off the main route to Granada.

In some respects Priego de Córdoba could be described as a town of contradictions. The little alleys of the old Hispano-Moorish district are so narrow that people are inclined to sidle rather than walk along them, whereas the Calle Río has all the trappings of prosperity — decorative wrought iron grilles, gleaming brass and passing traffic. At one end is the elderly Fuente del Rey, a conspicuous collection of statues, pools and water spouts. It is also a town where Baroque runs rampant, and seldom more riotously than in the churches. La Aurora is a case in point with its magnificent ceiling, disembodied cherubs, glistening altar and profusely embellished walls. The Church of La Asunción is another excellent example with its magnificent chapel of El Sagrario that has been declared a national monument.

The town grew rich with the demand for silk while the merchants flourished but fell on hard times again when the public suddenly decided that they preferred less expensive cotton to pure silk. The small local factories now move with the times and turn out shirts and other items of everyday wear demanded by their customers. The old town is essentially a place to wander about, inspecting the medieval castle, the decorative churches and the streets lined with antiquated houses. In the Calle Río a plaque draws attention to the family home of Niceto Alcalá Zamora who was President of the Second Spanish Republic before the outbreak of the Civil War. Anyone in search of a bed for the night has a choice of one or two small hotels and hostels but nothing in the upper price brackets.

There are some occasional diversions on the alternative route back to the capital as well as a secondary road to **Cabra**. Called *Egabro* in ancient times, it has a castle and the Church of San Juan Bautista, built in the twelfth century, which makes it one of the oldest churches in Andalucía. La Asunción has a rather splendid door complete with barley-sugar type marble pillars while the outlying sanctuary of the Virgen de la Sierra has a panoramic view.

A small turning off the Córdoba-Granada road takes in **Zuheros** which has the remains of a castle-fortress and the Neolithic cave of Los Murciélagos with a few prehistoric drawings and a collection of stalactites but nothing else very appealing unless one happens to be out in search of bats. Doña Mencía also has a ruined castle whereas **Baena** positively bristles with antiquated buildings. Palaces, churches, religious houses and old mansions jostle for position inside the protecting walls, along with the Torre del Sol and the 400 year-old Convent of Madre de Dios. Like its counterpart near Belalcázar, in the north of the province, it is much appreciated locally for the quality of its cakes. A little further up the road **Castro del Río** weighs in with a Roman bridge, which may have provided a right of way for Pompey before the battle of Monda, a couple of churches of no particular merit and a story about Cervantes in his capacity as a tax collector. Apparently he was accused of fiddling the grain returns in 1592 and tossed into a room in the town hall where he was kept prisoner for about a week — not the sort of incident to find a place in *Don Quixote*. Finally **Espejo** contributes an imposing fourteenth-century castle belonging to the Duke of Osuna and a small campsite for visitors who like the open-air life.

# 4

# *GIBRALTAR*

P olitically, as things stand at the moment, Gibraltar has no place
in a guide to Andalucía. However it is unquestionably of Spanish
origin, is firmly attached to the coastline of Cádiz and, barring a
spectacular act of God or another stupendous display of strength on
the part of Hercules, will always be an integral part of the Iberian
peninsula. As both The Rock and Spain are in the EEC it is logical to
assume that their differences will be settled eventually but, in the
meantime, they both maintain custom's posts on the border and
occasionally keep motorists hanging about for an hour or more, just
to show that they mean business. Nevertheless, in spite of these
aggravations there is a constant flow of traffic in both directions and
a surprising amount of quiet co-operation behind the scenes. Day
visitors are recommended to park on the Spanish side and walk in
over the airport's runway, or to take a taxi.

Gibraltar, known variously as Gib, The Rock and La Roca is
basically a gigantic chunk of limestone, 5km (3 miles) long and about
2km (1 mile) wide, rising to a height of 426m (1,396ft), with a sheer
drop on one side and a steep face on the other. Like any hill village
the town clings to the hem of its petticoats, dipping a nautical toe into
the waters of the Bay of Algeciras. Although the area is so small it
manages to cram in a whole variety of attractions, from wild flowers
and monkeys to a cable station at the summit and a handful of small,
sandy beaches.

The Rock has always been a bone of contention, simply because it
guards the straits separating Europe from Africa and the Mediterranean from the Atlantic. Some 40,000 years ago there were people
living in the large caves which, at different times, have served as food
stores, ammunition dumps, a proposed field hospital and a concert
hall. The Phoenicians knew it as *Calpe* before the Moors took pos-

*The Rock of Gibraltar*

*The quickest way up
and down!*

session in 711, renamed it *Gibel-el-Tarik* (Hill of Tarik) after their commander and guarded it ferociously with only an occasional setback for more than 700 years.

The Christians recaptured La Roca in 1462 on Saint Bernard's Day, so he was immediately appointed as its patron saint. However, during the Spanish War of Succession Gibraltar was captured by a Royal Naval force and 9 years later, under the Treaty of Utrecht, it was officially recognised as a British possession. Naturally the Spaniards refused to accept this decision and, with the help of the French, made determined efforts to recover it. The most memorable of these was the famous Great Siege, during which the defenders under General Elliot held out against all odds from 1779 to 1783.

Gibraltar played a vital role in both world wars, while Spain remained neutral but continued to resent the presence of foreigners on the door-step. Queen Elizabeth's official visit in 1954 irritated Franco to such an extent that he started to make life extremely difficult whenever possible and when The Rock was given a measure of self government he retaliated by closing the frontier on 23 June 1969. This fifteenth siege in its history was to be the longest of them all and even after the death of the dictator in 1975 it was some 10 years before normal relations were restored. In the meantime Gibraltar has become part of the EEC as a British Dependent Territory and was granted certain useful concessions, such as exemption from Value Added Tax, thereby increasing its reputation as a desirable shopping centre. However the war of words is still going on — Spain wants Gibraltar and The Rock wants to remain British, or at least independent.

Once across the border the first thing to be seen is the air terminal and beyond it the runway, starting from one side of the isthmus and continuing purposefully out to sea on the other. Quite apart from any delay caused by border controls road traffic plays second fiddle to aircraft and is forced to wait for flights taking off or landing at mercifully infrequent intervals every day. There are scheduled services to Britain and Tangier augmented by regular ferries to North Africa which leave from their own wharf, more or less level with the end of the runway. Behind this is the yacht basin, well protected from everything except the noise of planes, which is shared by the marinas and the local rowing club.

Winston Churchill Avenue makes a three-pronged attack on the town, changing its name to Smith Dorrien Avenue before it meets Main Street at Casemates Square. It is here, an hour before sunset, half a dozen times a year, that the governor is solemnly presented with three ceremonial keys and assured by the army that everything is in order and the fortress is secure. Casemates Gate marks the site of the old Moorish Water Gate where their galleys were launched in the days when the sea lapped up against the foot of the surrounding walls. It is only a stone's throw from the Fish Market Arch and another gateway, added by General Sir Robert Boyd in 1792 to facilitate the movement of stores from the supply ships to warehouses on the other side.

A somewhat unusual piece of military equipment can be seen on the way to Main Street, officially described as a Koelher Depression  Gun Carriage. It was apparently designed by a lieutenant in the Royal Artillery during the Great Siege to enable the defenders to deal with anyone who managed to dig trenches right up against the walls where they were out of the normal line of fire. Somewhat further on are the Grand Battery, a section of the Arab defences known in Spanish times as the Curtain of St Bernard, and the Land Port Gate where a drawbridge guarded the northern entrance to the Alcázar.

The first building of historic interest in Main Street is the **House of**  **Assembly** which started life as an Exchange in 1817 and rose to its present position as the home of the Gibraltar Parliament in 1969. Beyond it is the Cathedral of St Mary the Crowned, originally an  Arab mosque converted to Christianity by the Spanish in 1462. There are several other places of note in the vicinity, among them a monument to Queen Victoria and the Garrison Library, founded in 1793 and housed in an ancient building that replaced the home of the Spanish governors of La Roca. St Andrews Presbyterian Church and the Cathedral of the Holy Trinity, which served as a hospital in 1837, are quite close by, as is the Nefusot Yehudah Synagogue which had to be rebuilt after a disastrous fire in 1906.

Also on Line Wall Road, in the next block, is the **Gibraltar Museum** which has the remains of some Moorish baths in the basement  and was used to store bombs in the eighteenth century. Nowadays its main interests are history and archaeology with an enormous model of The Rock making it comparatively easy for visitors to follow the somewhat complicated details of its past life. Quite near by, and of special interest to Americans, is the archway monument designed by Dr Paul Gret of Philadelphia as a tribute to the combined British and USA forces stationed on The Rock during World War I.

In 1820 the old Judges Advocate Court House was replaced by the Supreme Court, created under charter from William IV. The building was restored in 1888 and has been the scene of a number of interesting cases. Probably the most baffling was the occasion on which it investigated, but failed to unravel, the mystery surrounding the ill-fated 'Marie Celeste', found abandoned with no apparent

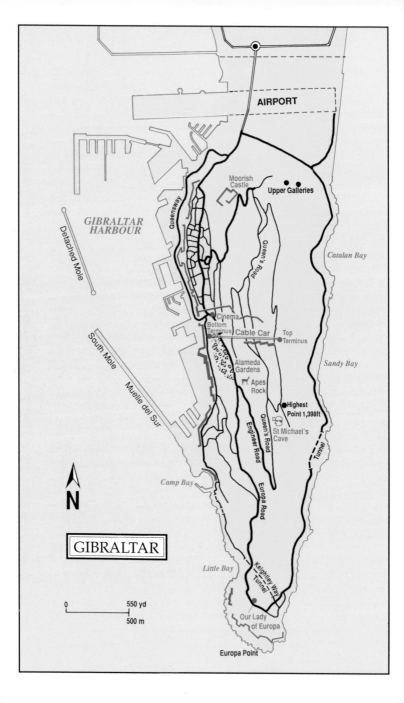

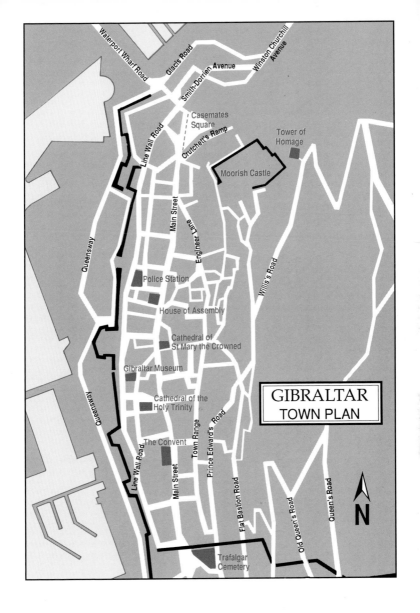

GIBRALTAR
TOWN PLAN

Waterport Wharf Road
Glacis Road
Smith-Dorrien Avenue
Winston Churchill Avenue
Line Wall Road
Casemates Square
Crutchett's Ramp
Tower of Homage
Moorish Castle
Main Street
Engineer Lane
Queensway
Willis's Road
Police Station
House of Assembly
Cathedral of St Mary the Crowned
Gibraltar Museum
Queensway
Cathedral of the Holy Trinity
Town Range
Prince Edward's Road
The Convent
Line Wall Road
Main Street
Flat Bastion Road
Old Queen's Road
Queen's Road
N
Trafalgar Cemetery

reason for the disappearance of her crew. One of the court's nearest neighbours is Government House where visitors can watch the weekly ceremonial Changing the Guard. It belonged to the Franciscan Order in the early sixteenth century and although it has been the official residence of every British Governor since 1710 it is still known to all and sundry as **The Convent**.

Beyond the medieval chapel of El Rosario a heavy gun keeps watch over the **South Port Gate**, originally a fortified entrance complete with a drawbridge, built in 1552 on the orders of Emperor Charles V. Somewhat incongruously it displays the coats-of-arms of Britain and Spain, co-existing peacefully side by side. The old wall was extended twice, once after a moderately successful attack by the pirate Barbarossa, and again when Philip II decided that it should be built right up to the top of the rock. The **Trafalgar Cemetery**, on the far side, dates back to the early eighteenth century and contains the graves of men who were injured during the Battle of Trafalgar and died of their wounds after being taken ashore. Nelson's body was also brought here before being taken back to England.

Although the main Police Station is of no particular interest from an architectural point of view, it is the headquarters of one of the oldest forces in the Commonwealth, having been founded in 1829, only a matter of weeks after London's Metropolitan Police Force came into being. The **Alameda Gardens**, beyond the cable car station, are Gibraltar's main recreation centre. They are full of trees and flowers with a lawn tennis club built over an old powder magazine and Crazy Golf laid out near the spot which was once set aside for public executions. There is also a refreshment kiosk, an open-air theatre and a modern casino with both gaming tables and slot machines as well as a bingo hall, a restaurant and a night club.

From the casino Europa Road follows a somewhat erratic course out to Europa Point with its red and white striped lighthouse and views across the straits to Ceuta and Tangier. Between these two is **Mons Abyla**, now known as Sidi Musa, or Apes Hill, which shares with Gibraltar the composite title of the Pillars of Hercules. Not far from the lighthouse there is a cricket ground and the shrine of Our Lady of Europa, much venerated by passing sailors. From here it is possible to follow the shoreline in either direction. Along the eastern side are the massive steel and concrete catchment areas which channel the precious rain-water down into vast storage tanks with a capacity of 13 million gallons. At each end of a clutch of rocky coves there is a small beach — Sandy Bay and Catalan Bay — with a hotel apiece while, a bit further on, Eastern Beach is larger, longer and noisier because it practically nudges the end of the airport runway.

The western route, with a shortcut through Keightley Way Tunnel, skirts past Little Bay and Camp Bay, two small beaches with sand and paddling pools but no accommodation, and eventually arrives at the Alameda Gardens.

Engineer Road, a left-hand fork off Europa Road just beyond the casino, is one of several routes up to the summit. Just short of the observation platform at Jews Gate it makes contact with Queen's Road which runs almost the whole length of the Upper Rock with breathtaking views across Algeciras Bay and down on to the harbour where toy-size ships move slowly in and out between the moles. It passes quite close to **St Michael's Cave**, a collection of subterranean grottoes with some very viewable stalactites and an underground lake that can be visited on request.

Beyond Haynes Cave, which has less to recommend it, the Old Queen's Road branches off on its own to visit the famous Barbary Apes. There can be very few people who have not heard of the legend that the British will only remain on The Rock as long as the apes are there. It may be nothing more than an old superstition but Winston Churchill took it seriously enough to ensure that the monkeys were well fed and protected throughout World War II. There was even a suggestion that some newcomers were brought over surreptitiously from North America, just to be on the safe side! Until recently they lived in complete freedom and enjoyed inspecting parked cars and accepting fruit and nuts from visitors . However, because tourists have been killing them with kindness in the form of unsuitable food, the apes are now segregated behind a barrier, out of harm's way.

The Old Queen's Road carries on down the mountainside, past the remains of the Moorish wall and through Devils Gap to reach the urban area. Meanwhile the 'new' version continues on its way to the **Upper Galleries**. These are a small section of the rabbit warren of underground tunnels that stretch for some 48km (30 miles). The original ones were part of a complicated defence system hewn out of solid rock during the Great Siege so that guns could be sited in commanding positions over-looking the isthmus connecting Gibraltar with the mainland. Anyone with enough energy can then set out on foot along Signal Station Road, past the upper cable car station to the highest point, and carry on down the Mediterranean Steps and Martins Way to Jews Gate. It is a long walk but well worth it for the views, especially as it is possible to pause for breath at the cable station where there is both a bar and a cafeteria.

Where motorists are concerned the road weaves its way down to the Moorish Castle, occupying a slightly lonely position above Tarik Passage. The **Tower of Homage** is all that remains of the Alcázar

*Ancient and modern in Gibraltar: the Moorish castle overlooking the marina and airport runway*

*Memorial to British and American forces of World War I*

built by the Arabs in 1333 on the site of an even earlier fortress. It is decidedly battle scarred but looks most impressive when it is floodlit and can be seen quite clearly from the other side of the bay. Several small alleys, often no more than steep stairways, lead back into the heart of the town.

Gibraltar is nothing if not cosmopolitan with distinctly British overtones. People of all colours, races and creeds live apparently quite happily side by side, the shops are full of merchandise from many different parts of the world while the restaurants and cafés will supply anything from roast beef to Indian curries, pizzas and chow mein. Although the best way to see Gibraltar is obviously on foot there are taxis for the asking, and as most of the drivers have a thorough working knowledge of the whole area they make ideal guides for sight-seers whose time is limited. The hotels range from large, comfort-able establishments with private swimming pools to compara-tively modest places which are quite acceptable. On the whole they tend to be a bit more expen-sive than their Spanish counter-parts just across the border.

*Gibraltar's famous apes used to roam freely but are now segregated*

Sports enthusiasts are cer-tainly well catered for with op-tions such as a windsurfing school at Eastern Beach that has facilities for water skiing as well, or diving holidays provided by Gibaqua, supervised by quali-fied instructors from the British Sub Aqua Club. Less ambitious holidaymakers can hire pedalos on any of the east facing beaches whereas sea trips are available for anyone who wants to go out in search of dolphins with the possibility of seeing an occa-sional shark or a white whale at close quarters. There is also some

*The strategic importance of the rock is shown by this preserved World War I gun at Devil's Steps Battery*

excellent fishing to be had, organised scenic tours of the The Rock by taxi or mini bus and opportunities to visit Tangier, either by plane or by ferry using a mini-liner which has drive-on drive-off facilities for passengers who want to take their own cars.

# 5

# *GRANADA*

---

The very name Granada has a magical quality about it. This is partly due, no doubt, to Washington Irving's *Tales of the Alhambra* which fill all the empty rooms and courtyards of the famous palace with legendary figures. The poet and dramatist Federico García Lorca also helped, as did Manuel de Falla, Victor Hugo, Andrés Segovia and Frank Sinatra. The Court of Lions is as instantly recognisable as the Tower of London, Sacre Coeur or the Statue of Liberty but, magnificent though it certainly is, the Alhambra is only an infinitesimal part of Granada.

The province is an oddly shaped area with a short Mediterranean coastline sandwiched in between Málaga and Almería. It shares a lengthy border with Jaén in the north and has just enough contact with Córdoba, Albacete and Murcia to justify mentioning them. The north-western sierras are pleasantly agricultural with small farms and isolated villages, fields of wheat, fruit trees and pastures strung out along the river courses. The Genil, in particular, has created a fertile valley on its way from the Sierra Nevada, past the capital and on through Córdoba to Sevilla where it joins the Gaudalquivir. To the north-east the outlook is completely different. The land becomes progressively more arid and unfriendly as it encroaches on the luna landscape of Almería before pushing on to the outer limits of Andalucía. Further south the foothills of the Sierra Nevada are tinged with pink in the spring when hundreds of almond trees suddenly burst into flower. They share the lower slopes with vineyards and citrus orchards that gradually give way to wooded hillsides covered with oaks, chestnuts and pines. On the opposite side of the range the spectacular mountain scenery of Las Alpujarras, described by the *Encyclopaedia Britannica* as having no parallel in Europe, links the shoreline with lofty peaks like Mulhacén and

Veleta, covered in perpetual snow.

The villages are spaced out fairly evenly all over the province. Most have something to recommend them, be it impressive scenery, ancient caves, Roman remains, Moorish fortresses or Christian castles and churches. In outlying areas the inhabitants are friendly without being effusive. There are quite a few hotels and hostels, although not many at the top end of the market apart from those in the capital, one each in Salobreña and Loja and a national *parador* up in the Sierra Nevada. It is also possible to find furnished apartments in the city and the coastal resort of Almuñécar in addition to more than a dozen campsites of varying descriptions. Granada has a local airport 4km (3 miles) from the capital on the main road to Sevilla and regular train services to Madrid, Sevilla, Córdoba, Algeciras and Almería. Buses connect the city with most places of interest in Andalucía as well as others further afield such as Barcelona, Murcia and Valencia. Motorists arriving under their own steam have a choice of major roads converging on the capital from Málaga, Sevilla, Córdoba, Jaén, Murcia and Almería with another that runs due south to join the coastal highway between Motril and Salobreña. The secondary roads are usually in quite good condition, especially the ones that search out and find the larger towns and villages. However it is as well to remember that the scenic route over the Sierra Nevada is a bit hairy as well as being impassable during the winter. Even as late as May the road up to the ski slopes of Solynieve can be icy in the early morning so anyone planning to set out at dawn or arrive late in the evening would be well advised to carry a set of chains. Cars are available for hire in both Granada and Almuñécar while energetic visitors without a licence can find bicycles in either centre as well as in Motril.

**Granada** is much more introspective than either Córdoba or Sevilla and even its festivals have a somewhat muted quality by comparison with those of its nearest neighbours. Ceremonies on the 1 and 2 January mark the anniversary of Ferdinand and Isabel's triumphant entry into the city. The Holy Week processions are essentially religious events as are the pilgrimages to Sacromonte Abbey in February in honour of St Cecil, the patron saint of the city, and to the Hermitage of St Michael on High on 29 September. This occasionally coincides with the Festival of Our Lady of Sorrows on the last Sunday of the month. On the other hand street corners are decorated with flowers on the Day of the Carnation which falls on 3 May and Corpus Christi is accompanied by bullfights, open-air entertainments and general rejoicing, followed by an International Music and Dance Festival which is held at the end of June or the

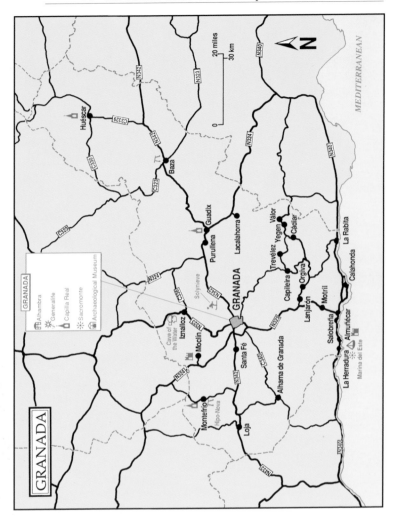

beginning of July.

Without any doubt the brightest jewel in Granada's crown is the **Alhambra**, the massive fortified palace built on the Assabica, or Red Hill, which dominates the old parts of the city. The site was chosen originally by both the Romans and the Visigoths and when the Moors had established residence Mohamed Ibn Alhamar decided that it was infinitely preferable to his own headquarters and moved

*The Alhambra,
the Court of Lions*

*The central
courtyard of
Charles V's
Palace, Granada*

all his goods and chattels across the Río Darro from the Albaicin.

Not a great deal remains of the early citadel apart from some walls and a few foundations, the towers overlooking the Cistern Court having been added much later, probably in about 1238. The Watch Tower, or Torre de la Vela, served a dual purpose, maintaining contact with outposts in the mountains and signalling the opening and closing of the water gates which controlled a complicated irrigation system by simply ringing the bell. Sentries stationed at the top had a splendid view of the whole area and visitors who clamber up these days insist that it is still just as impressive inspite of the smokey haze that often hangs over the city.

A tour of the Alhambra begins at the Puerta de las Granadas, a gateway built by Charles V, beyond which is a wooded area consisting mainly of pines and an elm grove planted by the Duke of Wellington when he had a spare moment during the Peninsular War. From here the road and a much shorter but uncomfortably steep footpath head for the Justice Gate whose tower once formed part of the inner ramparts. Beyond it is the Puerta del Vino where the local inhabitants used to collect their free wine and where the authorities now collect the visitors' entrance fees. To the left are the remains of the *alcazabar* with Charles V's palace on the right and, beyond it, the Moorish Alcázar, made largely of wood and plaster, which has captured the imagination of so many writers and yet can never be adequately described. It is ornate and yet amazingly simple, intricately carved with geometric patterns and texts from the Koran but completely devoid of statues because Islam forbids the use of figures of any kind.

Visitors are shown straight in to the Mexuar where palace officials conducted their everyday business but which was turned into a chapel by the Catholic Monarchs who added a small oratory at the far end with a view across to the Albaicin. On the other side of the adjoining Mexuar courtyard, with its small fountain and decorative walls, is the famous Court of Myrtles. This takes its name from the immaculate hedges on either side of a long, narrow pool running right down the middle, its mirror-like surface reflecting the slender columns that support the carved arches at each end. It was originally the central pivot of the State Apartments where the sultans held their official receptions and welcomed their most illustrious guests. The Barca Gallery leading off it separates the courtyard from the magnificent Hall of the Ambassadors which was once the throne room. Its domed ceiling is inlaid with stars and geometric patterns denoting the Seven Heavens of Islam, all clearly visible in the light from several pairs of horseshoe windows that pierce the decorated walls on the other three sides. There are a number of additional small chambers opening off the Court of Myrtles as well as an entrance into the empty crypt of Charles V's palace next door.

Beyond the Mocárabes Gallery, almost opposite, are the private apartments, the majority of them added by Mohammed V in the fourteenth century when he built the memorable Court of Lions. Its centrepiece is a round alabaster fountain surrounded by twelve of these sturdy grey marble animals that look much more like precocious cubs. It is enclosed on all sides with superbly carved arches supported by delicate pillars arranged singly or in pairs. The Abencerrajes Gallery, on the right hand side, was apparently the scene of a particularly unpleasant family massacre, although who was responsible for it is still a matter for conjecture.

The Kings Chamber is both decorative and slightly puzzling because the paintings, showing a variety of Moorish and Christian princely pastimes, are totally out of character. The Hall of the Two Sisters is typically Moorish in both design and execution, as is the Ajimeces Gallery separating it from the serene and lovely Daraxa Garden with its fountain and carefully located shrubs.

Outside the palace itself the Partal Gardens are terraced down to  the outer walls with their four small but superbly decorated towers. The Lady Tower dates from the fourteenth century and looks across the Río Darro far below to Sacromonte, whereas the Mihrab Tower and those of the Infantas and the Captives have an uninterrupted view of the Mountain of the Sun. It was here that the Nasrid kings built the **Generalife**, their unexpectedly restrained summer retreat, a few minutes' walk from the Alcázar along avenues fringed with oleanders and cypress trees. The buildings, though typical, are not particularly memorable but the gardens are a sheer delight and one which many visitors to the Alhambra miss altogether, perhaps because they are not pointed in that direction. As usual the constantly recurring theme is one of water.

Compared with all its Moorish neighbours the palace of Charles V looks rather grim and cumbersome and attracts plenty of criticism because he tore down a lot of the Alhambra to make room for it. The emperor, wanting a substantial and thoroughly durable palace commissioned Pedro Machuca, one of Michelangelo's pupils, in 1526 to design it for him. It was largely completed in the early seventeenth century although the final touches were only added quite recently.

The palace is simply a massive stone square with an enormous circular courtyard inside that has been used as both an arena and a bullring. There are some sculptured reliefs commemorating the emperor's most successful campaigns, as well as two separate museums. The Museum of Fine Arts on the upper floor traces the history of art in Granada, and is not particularly impressive, but the Museo Nacional de Art Hispano-Musulman is another matter altogether. It is full of items transferred from the Alhambra, along with other Moorish relics. Especially worth noting is a large blue amphora from the Hall of the Two Sisters, along with braziers and little pans that were used for burning perfumes.

Most of the ancient town which fitted into the vacant space at the far end of the Red Hill has now disappeared. However the few remaining buildings include the sixteenth-century Church of Santa María, built on the site of a much earlier mosque, and the former Convent of San Francisco which rose out of the remains of an Arab palace in 1495. Only a small part of the original building has been preserved, namely the main entrance, the tower and the temporary sepulchre where the Catholic Monarchs lay in state until they were moved to their own chapel adjoining the cathedral. The remainder has been rebuilt, restored, refurnished and converted into a *parador* which is small, atmospheric and very popular so, quite naturally, it is generally fully booked up months in advance.

Granada's cathedral, which claims to be among the most outstanding Renaissance churches in Spain, was built in the sixteenth and seventeenth centuries. The impressive façade was the work of Alonso Cano who also contributed a number of the paintings inside, complimented by original stained glass windows and an organ that was installed about 200 years afterwards. The cathedral museum turns out to be something of a disappointment unlike the **Capilla Real**, connected by a beautifully sculptured doorway in the south transept.

This royal chapel, which also has a separate entrance facing the old town hall, was completed in 1521. It is a rich and totally uninhibited tribute to the Catholic Monarchs, characterised by monograms and various coats-of-arms. A superb wrought iron grille by Master Bartolomé, protects the chancel with its regal mausoleums. The reclining statues are amazingly well preserved down to the minutest detail and give the impression of being faithful likenesses rather than sculptured images owing less to fact than to flattery. The bodies of Ferdinand and Isabel, their daughter and son-in-law, Juana the Mad and Philip the Fair, and their son Miguel are buried in the crypt below. Among other things the high altar portrays an incident during the siege of Granada while the sacristy is hung with some of the queen's favourite pictures and also contains her crown and sceptre and a sword that belonged to Ferdinand.

The **Palace of the Madraza**, facing the Capilla Real, was the original Moorish university. Later it became the city hall but has now
reverted to its academic status and is used mainly for lectures and
conferences. Charles V's university, founded in 1526, started life in
the Ecclesiastical Curia facing the cathedral across the Plazza Alonso
Cano. Nearly 250 years later it moved out to the ancient College of
San Pedro and its first home became the property of the church. It is
next door to the Archbishop's Palace which has its own collection of
religious paintings and works of art.

The **Corral del Carbón**, or Charcoal House, a block or two away off
the Calle Reyes Católicos, is the most elderly Moorish building still
standing in the city. It was a typical inn of its day, providing
accommodation for visiting merchants and a warehouse where they
could safely leave all the goods they carried with them. The Spaniards, who had no intention of encouraging trade in Granada, turned
it into a theatre, not unlike the famous Globe in London, with an open
pit area in the middle and covered balconies looking down on the
stage. These days it has taken on an entirely new role, providing
houseroom for a number of small shops selling local arts and crafts.

Carrying on round the foot of the Red Hill, the first place of interest
is the **Torres Bermejas**, an Arab fortress which has been guarding the
entrance to the Alhambra for the past 1,200 years. It has its own little
hill overlooking the Puerta de las Granadas on one side and the
Convent of Santa Catalina de Siena on the other. There are one or two
interesting churches in the vicinity, the most attractive being Santo
Domingo, which was once part of the Monastery of Santa Cruz la
Real, founded by the Catholic Monarchs in 1504. It is only slightly
older than the Church of St Cecilio in the Campo del Príncipe, home
of the city's patron saint who makes a ceremonial pilgrimage to
Sacromonte Abbey on his feast day every year. Somewhat further on
is the beautiful walled mansion that belonged to Manuel de Falla, full
of memorabilia of one of Spain's most famous composers who died
in 1946. Finally, standing on its own, surrounded by trees with an
ornamental lake for company, the small but delightful Carmen de los
Mártires, or Villa of the Martyrs, is at home to visitors on Sundays.

The Río Darro or the part that has not been covered over separates
the Alhambra from the Albaicin. This ancient falconers' quarter is
lightly peppered with memorable buildings and still retains a slight
flavour of its Moorish ancestry. The oldest survivors, both dating
from the eleventh century, are the ruined Puente del Cadi, or the
Bridge of the Judge, which was demolished in the mid-seventeenth
century, and the Arab baths on the Calle del Darro, fully and expertly
restored in 1928. Among their most immediate neighbours, facing on

to the same street, is the **Casa de Castil**, an exuberantly decorated sixteenth century mansion which belonged to Bernando de Zafra, a one-time secretary at the court of Ferdinand and Isabel. It is worth seeing for its unusual stone carvings, including such things as flying scallop shells, and also because it is now Granada's main Archaeological Museum. The earliest exhibits were discovered in some of the prehistoric caves that are a little-known feature of the province, while others were discarded by the Iberians in the days before the Romans overran their settlements. One of its most interesting features is a unique collection of Egyptian funeral urns. However, from a less specialised point of view, the section devoted to Moorish art is probably more popular.

Other buildings in the immediate area also have something of interest to offer. For example, the **Convento de Santa Catalina de Zafra** is built round a small Moorish house of somewhat uncertain ancestry. It may well date from about the eleventh century and there must have been a logical reason for preserving it when the convent was founded in 1520. Only a block or so away is the Church of San Pedro, one of the most traditional examples of its kind, where a flamenco mass is conducted on the third Sunday of every month.

From here a choice of little streets lead up from the Road of the Sad Ones through the Albaicin to **Sacromonte**. This is an area which is best explored at leisure, springing quite a few surprises in the form of ancient Arab fountains, typical Moorish houses, old understated churches and a few remnants of the original fortifications. The main things to look out for are the Church of the Saviour in a square of the same name, and the Mirador de San Nicolás, both of which have glorious views of the Alhambra backed by the snowy peaks of the Sierra Nevada. Also worthy of attention is the Convento de Santa Isabel la Real in the street of San Juan de los Reyes. There are still some traces of the Moorish palace that was knocked down to make way for the convent, founded in memory of the Catholic queen after her death in 1504.

The Puerta de Elvira, once the main entrance to the city, is one of the few ancient gateways to have survived, along with the Puerta Monaita, the nearby Las Pesas Arch and some very disjointed sections of the outer defences. Beyond them is Sacromonte with its own dilapidated walls and cave dwellings where the gipsy community have been living for several hundred years. Quite a number of these hill homes, decorated with pictures, ceramics and polished metalware, have been redesigned in order to part gullible tourists from their money. Passers-by are invited inside to watch a flamenco show, the children are sent out to buy wine at greatly inflated prices, grandmothers are instantly available for a spot of fortune telling and eventually the guests are sent back to their hotels certainly poorer if no wiser for their experiences. However, provided the visitor is fully aware of all these pitfalls it can be a very pleasant and entertaining way of spending an odd hour or two. Unfortunately Sacromonte Abbey is not open to the public except for the festival of San Cecilio.

There are other places worth visiting on the opposite side of the Gran Vía de Colón, an arrow-straight boulevard that was driven in an arbitary fashion through the old quarter during the nineteenth century. Among them is the lavishly decorated **Church of San Juan de Dios** with a large tiled dome that makes it quite easy to locate. The interior is dominated by an enormous gilt altarpiece containing a gold and silver door behind which is the tomb of St John of God who founded the Order of the Knights Hospitallers as well as the ancient hospital just down the road. A block or two away the remains of El Gran Capitán are buried infront of the high altar in the Church of San Jerónimo. Having admired both the tomb and the fine altarpiece visitors are shown round two beautifully restored patios in the monastery and invited to inspect the contents of its small museum.

A good deal further away, near the Acera de Darro, is the Church of Our Lady of Sorrows, an eighteenth-century building profusely decorated with marble, which is the shrine of the patroness of Granada. It is just off the Carrera del Genil, a very popular spot with people who enjoy open-air markets, and only a block or two from the picturesque Río Genil. On the far side of the bridge, and a short walk along the opposite bank, is the Hermitage of San Sebastian, an Arab meeting place from the thirteenth century where Boabdil finally came to terms with the Catholic Monarchs in 1492. Two other outlying attractions are the Huerta de San Vicente in Arabial Street, once the home of Federico García Lorca, the poet and dramatist who was shot out of hand by Franco's troops during the Civil War, which includes a small museum, and secondly the magnificent Carthusian Monastery on the road to Alfacar.

Granada's main shopping centre consists of a maze of narrow pedestrian walkways, occasionally shared with donkeys, grouped round the Plaza Bibarrambla within easy reach of the cathedral. It spills out into the Alcaicera, a thriving silk market in Moorish times which was destroyed by fire about 150 years ago. It was restored along very similar lines and, rather surprisingly, manages to create a fairly authentic atmosphere, although what must have been typical individual bazaars are now filled with expensive glass and china, antiques and rather tawdry souvenirs.

The nearby Casa de los Tiros, in the Plaza del Padre Suárez, houses both the tourist office and the Museum of History and Handicrafts. It is quite an impressive sixteenth-century building complete with towers and battlements, stone carvings, statues and the Venegas coat-of-arms. The museum, which is being refurbished, traces the history of the city.

Granada is still very much a university town, with students accounting for about one sixth of the population, but it is also becoming increasingly tourist conscious. There are several first class hotels including the *parador* and a long list of other comfortable ones as well as a selection of inexpensive hostels and small establishments. Parking can sometimes be quite a problem and it is often necessary to find somewhere to eat in the vicinity even if breakfast is available on the premises. There are a few good restaurants and several perfectly acceptable ones in addition to a whole host of small bars serving snacks with the drinks. Most of these *tapas* are varied but quite predictable although occasionally they may include such things as fieldfares fried with garlic, soused anchovies, pork on the bone or partridges with lettuce.

Souvenir hunters have a wide variety of local crafts to choose from, which can be found in a great many small shops throughout the old quarters. Anyone on the lookout for choice pieces is likely to find them at the National Company of Handicrafts in the Corral del Carbón. Sporting enthusiasts are just as well catered for with more than a dozen different swimming pools in and around the capital in addition to the National Rifle Range, the Royal Tennis and Show-jumping Societies, a sailing club, a well-equipped stadium and the University Sports Club.

The main road from Granada to the east climbs up steeply out of the capital, crossing the Río Darro and skirting the foothills of the Sierra Nevada on its way to Guadix. As the landscape begins to flatten out more and more small buildings appear along the roadside fronted by pottery of every description; jugs and jars, pots and plates, with highly coloured selections attached to large wire screens that show them off to good advantage. The distances separating these wayside shops gradually get smaller until they disappear altogether in the village of **Purullena** where the displays present a united front with the addition of brass and copper to reflect the sun and catch the eye of passing motorists. Although they build small houses for their merchandise, and in some cases even live over the shop, a great many local inhabitants prefer the cave dwellings cut back into the red clay hillsides all around. These days the white painted doors may well be protected by a porch or even a garden with space for the car and the chimneys protuding like mushrooms through the scrub overhead,

*Purullena: local pottery for sale along the roadside*

are far less obtrusive than the television aerials that keep them company.

**Guadix**, a little further up the road, also has its hill houses but they are rather tucked away on the outskirts of the town. Most of the occupants live in them from choice, pointing out that they are cool in summer, warm in winter and the roofs never leak. The habit is said to have started in earnest when the Moors went to ground to avoid the unwelcome attentions of Philip II and found it so convenient that they never thought of moving out again. Instead they have updated their homes and found suitable caves for a small chapel as well as little bars and discos.

The site has been occupied since prehistoric times and was an important road junction in the days of the Romans and the Visigoths because then, as now, it marked the spot where the roads from Murcia and Almería joined forces for the final run into Granada. It was also a lucrative mining centre producing copper, iron and silver which endeared it to both Hannibal and the Emperor Augustus who founded a local settlement and called it *Acci*.

Like all the other towns in Andalucía Guadix was taken over by the Moors in the eighth century and, after renaming it *Wadi Ash*, they quite naturally built themselves a large *alcazabar*, which the Chris-

83

tians restored when they eventually captured the town in 1489. The equally imposing cathedral dates from roughly the same time and was designed in part by Diego de Siloé who is also believed to have been responsible for the elaborate doorway of the convent church of Santiago. Quite apart from its other attractions the cathedral has a collection of priceless manuscripts, relics of St Torcuato and some memorable works of art tucked away in the museum. Other places of interest in the town include three fortified gateways with part of the old ramparts still attached and the sixteenth-century Mudéjar Church of Saint Anne. Some of Guadix's citizens have achieved a certain degree of fame, among them the conquistador Pedro de Mendoza, who established a colony on the River Plate in South America and christened it Nuestra Señora Santa María del Buen Aire, to be abbreviated later to Buenos Aires.

Anyone taking the right-hand fork to Almería with a bit of time to spare might well deviate slightly from the main road to visit **Lacalahorra**. It is a fairly typical little village, nestling at the foot of a vast, gently-sloping mound that looks a bit like a gigantic tortoise that has fallen asleep at the edge of the plains with an ancient castle on its back. The palace is a rather splendid affair with a domed tower at each corner, graceful arcades surrounding the central patio, fine carving round the windows and an elegant staircase leading up to the balustrade. Conversely, motorists on their way to Murcia will find the ruins of an Arab fortress in **Baza** about 50km (31 miles) away. Both larger towns have a sprinkling of hotels and hostels which are by no means exceptional but do perfectly well for the night.

Both Baza and **Huéscar** have their own troglodyte communities to which the latter adds the Theatre of Huéscar, that is, in fact, a convent in the Square of Santo Domingo, and the Parish Church of St Mary the Elder dating from the end of the fifteenth century. It is a pleasant understated building with a number of ancient treasures, the most valued of which is a shrine known as the Little Tower of Art. Among the town's other attractions are a few cave paintings, some Roman mosaics, the Tutugi necropolis and the remnants of its *alcazabar*. It also has the unusual distinction of having been at war with Denmark for nearly 200 years because it omitted to sign a peace treaty after the Peninsular War. This was rectified quite recently and Danish visitors to Granada are welcome there.

A series of small roads amble quite aimlessly through the country-side bordering on Jaén, calling at several totally forgettable little villages until one of them finally makes its way to **Iznalloz**. This is another hill town with Roman associations and Moorish remains in addition to a wayside inn and the archaeologically interesting Cave of the Water which can be visited on request, but only after a long, hard climb. Nor is there anything of particular interest further to the west apart from Moclin, a Nasrid outpost which has preserved some of its walls and an ancient castle as well as the highly regarded Sanctuary of Christ of the Cloth.

From here a minor road joins the main highway to Jaén just short of Pinos Puente, complete with its Roman bridge, standing four square in the fertile Vega de Granada. Not far away, on the route linking Granada with Málaga, is the ancient town of **Santa Fé**. It marks the site of a burned out encampment used by Ferdinand and Isabel during the last phase of their reconquest of Andalucía and where the agreement giving Columbus the green light for his first voyage across the Atlantic was signed. At each end of the two major thoroughfares, set out in the form of a cross, is a fortified gateway — called respectively Granada, Loja, Sevilla and Jaén — built by the Catholic Monarchs in 1491.

A few kilometres before the border which Granada shares with Málaga and Córdoba, the town of **Loja** is a good place to stop, especially for anyone staying at the Finca La Bobadilla, one of the few five-star hotels in the province. It is situated out in the countryside north of the town and provides its guests with every luxury at prices not everybody can afford. There are some less expensive hotels and hostels and a handful of quite reasonable restaurants much closer to all the various urban attractions. These include the ninth-century *alcazabar* that has been declared a national monument, the Santa Clara monastery and the Church of San Gabriel, attributed in part to Diego de Siloé who also left his mark on the cathedrals of Granada and Málaga. The Río Genil runs sedately through the town after taking a spectacular tumble over the Infiernos Falls and then continues in a leisurely fashion northwards to lose itself temporarily in the large Iznajar reservoir.

**Montefrío**, north-east of the lake, along a secondary road off the main route to Córdoba, offers three quite different tourist attractions. The oldest of these by a long way is Hipo-Nova, the sparse remains of an ancient settlement with an Iberian acropolis and a collection of dolmens at Peña de los Gitanos, or Gipsy Rock, 4km (2 miles) outside the town. The old Church of Santa María dates from the fifteenth century and was built on the site of an Arab fortress where King Aben-Ismael III once held court. Although the Church of the Incarnation is considerably younger it is rather more interesting because, instead of being the conventional shape, the eighteenth-century architect decided to make it round and this created certain problems with the interior decorations and produced unusual sound effects.

To the south of the Sierra de Loja, with its bubbly collection of hills and evenly spaced olive trees, the Embalse de los Bermejales is a favourite haunt of fishermen in search of carp while **Alhama de Granada** busies itself with people who are anxious to do something about their rheumatic twinges. The ancient Moorish baths are still in operation and, to make things easier for the patients, a comfortable hotel has been built over the top of them. Anyone who is only there for the view can explore the surrounding countryside or visit the Church of the Incarnation in the centre of the town.

As the few roads to the south are small, shortlived and in some places almost impassable the only route to the coast is quite time consuming. Motorists are forced to drive back towards the capital when two options are open to them. One is via Gabia la Grande which takes great pride in a fourth-century underground chamber left behind by the Romans and a somewhat younger Arab tower. Alternatively a rather hairy shortcut from Mala links up with the main route to Motril just north of the Puerto del Suspiro del Moro.

Almost immediately a fork to the right provides a scenic alternative to the main road, twisting and turning through the Sierra del Chaparral to **Almuñécar**, the largest of Granada's coastal resorts. The town is said to have been founded by the Phoenicians and a

*Almuñécar: the modern sea front east of the old town*

*The Marina del Este near Almuñécar*

collection of ruins enclosed in gardens behind the headland are believed by some local people to be the remains of cellars where they stored their salt. The Cave of the Seven Palaces, an enormous water storage tank, is also attributed to the Phoenicians whereas the Romans contributed an odd structure known as the Monk's Tower and two interlocking viaducts on the outskirts. The castle, dominating the headland separating two different bays, is a comparative newcomer to the scene. It took the place of an Arab fortress in the time of Charles V, with a massive square tower known as La Mazmorra and an ancient graveyard immediately next door. The hillside below is saturated with small, secretive white houses lining the narrow cobbled streets where there is only just enough space for an expert driver to squeeze past in a fairly modest car.

In complete contrast the seafront is a jumbled mass of lofty apartment blocks interspersed with small shops and restaurants and empty spaces that are being blasted into submission ready for more highrise buildings which will eventually overlook the promenade and the long stretch of rather greyish sand. So far the hotels are fairly basic without being downright uncomfortable and much the same can be said for the restaurants and cafés, several of which tend to hibernate during the winter. Furnished apartments are the best bet for visitors planning to stay for a week or more, with facilities for shopping in the covered market, any of a number of grocery shops that call themselves supermarkets or the weekly outdoor variety held every Friday quite close to the beach. It is possible to hire a car, a moped or a bicycle, which comes in useful for anyone who wants to take advantage of the various sports activities up and down the coast.

A case in point is **La Herradura**, a small village almost on the border with Málaga which has an underwater fishing and diving school. There are plenty of opportunities for windsurfing and even water skiing with a parachute as well as fishing or simply taking a  chair and a sun umbrella down on to the beach. The **Marina del Este**, slightly closer by sea than it is by road, is one of the prettiest marinas on the Costa del Sol. It is tucked in under the hillside, protected from bad weather, with a delightful waterside complex that includes a small hotel. The most popular evening entertainment is the Saturday night flamenco show at the Venta Luciano where the entrance fee includes a buffet supper and plenty of local wine. It is about 3km (2 miles) inland from Almuñécar.

Eastwards from Almuñécar the road follows the coastline round to **Salobreña**, another ancient settlement that was well known to the Phoenicians. Its typical white houses scramble up the hillside to the Moorish Alcázar which was neglected after the reconquest of Andalucía but has now been fully restored. The leading hotel, with its facilities for tennis and swimming, has a site all to itself on the top of a nearby cliff, in addition to which there are one or two modest inns and half a dozen restaurants in the vicinity, as well as a local campsite. From here it is only 4km (2 miles) to **Motril**, a fairly busy commercial port interested mainly in sugar cane and chemicals. However it also has a clutch of unremarkable hostels, a sixteenth-century church built on Moorish foundations, the hilltop Sanctuary of Our Lady of the Head and a golf course which it shares with Salobreña.

Beyond Motril the coastal highway continues to keep company with the sea, exploring various little headlands, most of them sporting an ancient watch tower that has seen far better days. These large, round, stone lookouts are a feature of the Costa del Sol, some of them preserved as ancient monuments, others utilised as outbuildings at the edge of a small property while the rest are left to moulder all alone as they have been doing for centuries. A number of the coves are occupied by small seaside resorts, like Calahonda or Castell de Ferro, which may or may not possess a local inn and an adjacent campsite. The last-but-one village on the Granada side of the border with Almería is La Rabita where a secondary road heads up into Las Alpujarras, a little known but magnificently scenic region of the Sierra Nevada.

From Albuñol, some 10km (6 miles) inland, the larger of two roads continues to swerve, double back on itself and change its mind again, leaving its smaller companion to do the best it can on the way past the Venta del Tarugo to Cádiar. For most people the first option will obviously be preferable, especially as it arrives eventually at **Orgiva**, the main town in the area. It is a pleasant enough little place with its full quota of olives and orange trees and a parish church that has both a fifteenth-century altarpiece and a much revered Christ of the Expiration carved by Martínez Montañés. However **Lanjarón**, practically next door, does rather better where hotels are concerned simply because it is a well known spa. The natural springs are said to cope manfully with everything from liver complaints and digestive problems to arthritis and nervous tension. As there is a great deal of surplus water about, large quantities are bottled and sold all over Spain. The town is conveniently placed about 50km (31 miles) from the capital, just off the main highway to Motril.

**Las Alpujarras** is a totally fascinating area which has only quite ✳ recently come to terms with the twentieth century. Although most of these villages can now be reached by car the best way to explore the region is either on foot or on horseback. Special riding holidays are arranged, lasting for several days, with overnight stops at Spartan wayside inns where neither the facilities nor the food have changed to any great extent.

From Orgiva a pleasantly scenic route fiddles its way through the mountains and across the moorlands to **Cádiar** where the fountain runs with wine in the main square during the October festival and where the second Alpujarras revolt is believed to have started. Further to the east **Valor** goes one better, recreating the battle for its local castle with the Christian and Islamic forces, all in appropriate costumes, fighting for possession of a wooden replica specially designed for the occasion.

A few kilometres away is **Yegen** where the English author Gerald Brenan lived for 7 years collecting material for his classic book *South from Granada* which makes compulsive reading for anyone who intends to do more than just drive through the area. It is an atmospheric village with a very basic inn, plenty of olive and almond trees and a view across the arid Sierra de Gador to the Mediterranean.

**Trevélez**, reputed to be the highest village in Spain, is a trifle out of the way up a narrow river valley in the shadow of Mulhacén, the snow-capped peak that was named after Muley Hacén who ruled Granada in the fifteenth century. It is known principally for its snow-cured hams which can be seen hanging in modern drying sheds. The village itself is almost unchanged with a huddle of white sugar-cube houses and a maze of steep, narrow alleys less suited to cars than to all the various animals which insist of having the right of way.

**Capileira**, on the other hand, has set its sights on becoming a popular holiday resort with nothing so far in the way of hotels but some beautiful scenery, a small local museum and a road, passable only at the height of the summer, across the top of the Sierra Nevada to the ski resort of Solynieve on the other side. A short distance from the village is the Buddhist sanctuary of O-Sel-Ling, named as the Place of Clear Light by the Dalai Lama during a visit in 1982. Anyone in search of utter solitude can retreat briefly to one of the tiny stone huts built on the mountainside by the resident monks.

Travellers who are less anxious to leave the world behind should find what they are looking for at the delightful **Villa Turistica de Bubión**, slightly to the south. It is more like a miniscule modern suburb attached to an old Berber village with furnished studios and villas equipped with open log fires and a restaurant at the hotel for anyone who does not want to cook or to try out a bar in the adjacent hamlet. One of the last places on the way back to Lanjarón via this northern route is **Soportújar**, ideally placed for visitors who feel inclined to explore the National Park of the Sierra Nevada with its oaks and chestnut trees, bird life, deer and mountain goats, trout-filled streams and impressive views.

Whereas the Las Alpujarras region is seen to best advantage in the spring and early autumn, Solynieve is first and foremost a winter sports resort. Most of the hotels, apart from the *parador*, take their own holidays from May to November, regardless of the fact that a modicum of skiing is possible throughout the summer. There are chair lifts and a cable car from the lower slopes at **Prado Llano**. Once up at the Borreguiles level T-bars and chair lifts can transport some 20,000 people an hour up to the Veleta peak where expert skiers have a choice of more than thirty runs including an almost verticle slope with trails covering some 10km (6 miles) down into the valley. The whole complex also caters also for those who do not wish to ski and is only about an hour's run from Granada, provided the road is clear of ice and snow.

# 6

# *HUELVA*

Huelva, tucked away at the western extremity of Andalucía, receives fewer foreign visitors than most of the other provinces regardless of its many and varied attractions. It shares a common frontier with Portugal, marked by the Río Guadiana. To the north, beyond the foothills of the Sierra Morena, is Extremadura, the land of the Conquistadores who appropriated vast tracts of the New World for Spain in the sixteenth century. In the east the region is bounded by the province of Sevilla and cut off from Cádiz by the marshy delta of the Río Guadalquivir which has been converted into one of Europe's leading nature reserves.

The north of the province is a delightful expanse of rolling hills and forests full of oak, chestnut and walnut trees and dotted here and there with mouldering and frequently extremely ancient fortresses. This gradually levels out, giving way to the darker green of eucalyptus, to orchards full of cherries, pears and apples, agricultural areas and vineyards, many of which have been uprooted to make way for massive strawberry beds. Pines, with some help from palms and citrus trees, fringe the Atlantic seaboard, memorable for its seemingly endless stretches of unspoiled golden sands. Plans are afoot to turn some of the little isolated fishing villages into holiday resorts although the powers-that-be are determined not to allow them to develop into the glass and concrete tourist warrens that have robbed part of the Mediterranean coast of its essential character.

Huelva has not always been one of Andalucía's poor relations. There are several good reasons for believing that it was part of the legendary kingdom of *Tartessus*, not least among them the discovery of a stone carving, dating from around 700BC and known as the Mask of Tharsis, which some experts think may be a likeness of King Arganthonius. There were thriving communities in the region during the Bronze Age, the Greek and Phoenician traders were regular visitors and the Celts established their town of *Ilipla* at Niebla, only to have it captured by the Romans in 194BC. The area went from strength to strength during the Roman occupation, was highly thought of by the Visigoths and respected by the Moors who granted it the status of a kingdom in the eleventh century. The port of *Onuba*, later to be rechristened Huelva, handled most of the trade between Al-Andalus and North Africa, accumulating even greater wealth and prestige in the process.

Despite its long history **Huelva**, the capital city and once again a busy port, has very little to show from the past. This is mainly because all the old buildings were destroyed in the earthquake of 1755 which devastated Lisbon. A few modest attempts were made to repair the damage — the Church of San Pedro was restored on the site of an ancient mosque, the sixteenth-century Church of La Concepción rebuilt and the Convent of La Merced transformed into a cathedral. Among the more modern innovations worth mentioning is the Barrio Obrero, or Workers' Quarter, built by the Río Tinto mining company for its employees which, in consequence, owes rather more to suburbia than it does to Spain. On the other hand the Archaeological Museum has collected a whole range of exhibits.

The capital keeps in touch with the rest of the country by means of regular train services to Sevilla and Madrid with connections to centres like Granada, Barcelona and Almería. Buses operate throughout the province, augmented by long-distance coach links with Granada and Cádiz. There are plenty of taxis for shorter journeys, which will also undertake longer trips when it is essential to agree the fare in advance, and cars can be hired by visitors who prefer to explore under their own steam. The main roads are generally in good condition, especially the Huelva-Sevilla highway and a splendid new route northwards to Extremadura through the Sierra de Aracena, largely completed in 1991. The secondary roads can be suspect in places, particularly if maintenance work is going on and byways are unpredictable.

Accommodation varies nearly as much as the road surfaces and falls into almost identical categories. At the moment there are only two *paradores*, one at Ayamonte and the other on the coast near Mazagón, both of them comfortable but of no historic interest whatsoever. Huelva city boasts one first class hotel and several less up-market establishments ranging from one to three stars while further afield there are three star hotels in Almonte, Palos de la Frontera, Ayamonte and Punta Umbría.

Most people, unless they happen to be in Huelva on business, prefer to stay out of town and as **Punta Umbría** is the nearest seaside resort to the capital this is an obvious choice. It is a typical fishing village that has turned itself into a popular holiday playground and lies about 20km (12 miles) away on the far side of the Río Odiel. It boasts a choice of hotels, some of which are fairly basic, a selection of restaurants and cafés and an official campsite for tents and caravans. The beaches, overlooked by an ever-increasing number of private villas, are extensive enough not to be too crowded during the summer and are all but deserted at the end of the season. There are facilities for all types of water sports , although the golf course is at Aljaraque, some 14km (9 miles) away on the road to the capital.

From Punta Umbría a secondary road follows the sand dunes along the coastline through El Portil to **El Rompido**, a cheerful little place with a pleasant campsite and a large oyster breeding complex established by the Aguas del Pino marine research centre. It is a comparatively recent venture by the Andalucían authorities and is intended to introduce an entirely new industry to the area.

The Río Piedras which meets the sea near El Rompido forces the road inland to **Cartaya**, on the main road to Ayamonte. At first sight there is nothing particularly memorable about it but anyone with the time and inclination to inspect the village more closely will be rewarded with the ruins of a Roman castle, the fifteenth-century Mudéjar hermitage of La Consolación and the Church of San Pedro. It has two modest hotels and a restaurant which is close to the railway crossing.

Further to the west, and also on the main road, is the thriving little town of **Lepe**, famous for its melons, figs and strawberries to which have been added water melons, asparagas beds and citrus orchards. Like Cartaya it has two small hotels but no castle or campsite. The fifteenth-century church of Santo Domingo de Guzmán is usually open to visitors, many of whom make a point of being there a week after Whitsun for the Virgen de la Bella pilgrimage.

Beyond the intensely cultivated area round Lepe the main highway heads straight for Ayamonte with side roads branching off seawards to isolated hamlets like La Antilla which have little of interest for the average tourist. On the other hand **Isla Cristina**, separated from the mainland by a series of canals, has some splendid beaches, a handful of typical holiday hotels at the lower end of the market and an energetic fishing fleet. For locals and visitors alike there are plenty of fish to be caught in the Carreras estuary and a modicum of shooting in the surrounding area, provided one has the necessary licence.

**Ayamonte** is another fishing village which has expanded rapidly in an attempt to become a popular holiday resort and is still building. At the moment its main claim to fame is that of a frontier post from which an elderly ferry transports cars and foot passengers across the Río Guadiana to Vila Real de Santo Antonio in Portugal, watched over by customs officials every day throughout the year. However things are bound to change somewhat when the new suspension bridge is open and a four-lane highway bypasses the town.

In the meantime the Parador Costa de la Luz is a favourite stopping place for motorists on their way to the Algarve. The town boasts some half dozen other hotels of various sorts and descriptions and a few restaurants including the Casa Barberi which guarantees that its *paella* and other traditional dishes are as good today as they were when it first opened in 1917. There is not a great deal to see in the way of old buildings apart from the Church of San Francisco and its slightly older sister church of Nuestra Señora de las Angustias, dedicated to the patron saint of the town.

North of the Huelva-Ayamonte highway is **Villablanca**, not a very prepossessing old village where the sixteenth-century church, dedicated to the local patron saint, is rather less interesting than the remains of some ancient windmills, far removed from their famous cousins in La Mancha. Most of the hamlets hereabouts have some elderly relic with which to attract any tourists who happen to be passing by. **Sanlúcar de Guadiana** has both the river and a ruined castle, **Villaneuva de los Castillejos** weighs in with a hermitage and a mildly viewable parish church while **San Bartolomé de la Torre** lays its history on the line with a dolmen, the remains of a Punic tower and some slight but convincing evidence that the Romans once settled there. A quite acceptable road rejoins the highway at Gibraleón which has made a reasonably good job of preserving part of its original walls and a number of antiquated buildings. San Juan, one of three different churches, occupies the site of a mosque which in turn replaced a temple built by the Visigoths. From here it is a short, easy run back to the capital.

The coast to the east of Huelva city has even more to offer once you are clear of the area occupied almost exclusively by petro-chemical companies. At the Punta del Sebo, where the Río Odiel and the Río Tinto join forces for their final journey to the sea, there is a massive statue of Christopher Columbus. The **Monasterio de Santa María de la Rábida**, where Christopher Columbus spent 7 years planning and organising his voyage, is not a very impressive building. It is somewhat Moorish in character with bare white walls and a red tiled roof, standing in spacious gardens. Just inside the grounds is a tall, pillar-like monument which was erected a century ago to the men

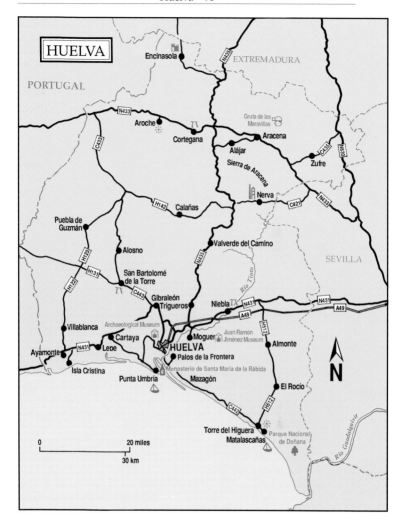

who had sailed westwards 400 years before in the hope of finding a new sea route to India. Part of the monastery has been set aside as a museum with guided tours each morning and afternoon. Nearly everything in the museum is labelled in four languages, including English, which makes it much easier to appreciate all the treasures on display.

The tour of the monastery includes the Mudéjar Cloister, dating from the fourteenth century, and the more recent Claustro de la Hospedería, filled with flowering plants, as well as the main church and the Chapel of the Virgin. Many of the frescoes are a comparatively recent addition by Vázquez Días. The alabaster statue of Santa María de la Rábida, also known as Our Lady of Miracles is not particularly beautiful. She stands surrounded by all the appropriate insignia with the three caravels in full sail at her feet. The monastery has a restaurant and a small but comfortable hostel for visitors.

The little port of **Palos de la Frontera** silted up a long time ago but it still preserves a much restored and decidedly dry Roman well where legend insists that Columbus and his crews took on water for their epic voyage. Nearby is the Church of San Jorge where they gave thanks for their safe return and where, some 35 years later, Hernan Cortéz is said to have prayed for God's blessing before he left to conquer Mexico. The town's other main attractions are a marble statue of Martín Alonso Pinzón, the second most important figure who took part in the expedition to San Salvador, and the family home in the main street of the town.

**Moquer**, another one-time port has a less dramatic history but rather more in the way of ancient buildings. Foremost among them are the fourteenth-century convent of Santa Clara and the fractionally younger Corpus Christi Chapel which was originally part of the local hospital. It is an attractive little town which hit the headlines when the poet Juan Ramón Jiménez was awarded a Nobel Prize in 1956. His home has been turned into a museum, full of memorabilia and enthusiastic press cuttings, while a second museum is concerned mainly with religious art. The two villages have about a dozen hotels between them and are surrounded by fields of strawberries.

Back on the coast, where the long sandy beaches of the Costa de la Luz are some of the most beautiful to be found anywhere in Spain, there are only two resorts worth mentioning at the moment. The first is **Mazagón**, surrounded by pine trees and totally absorbed in the business of catering for holidaymakers. It is comparatively quiet and unassuming although it is still expanding with a keen eye to the future, encouraged originally by the celebrations marking the 500th anniversary of the discovery of the Americas. The only hotel of any note is the Parador Nacional Cristóbal Colón about 6km (4 miles) up the coast, standing alone overlooking the beach with its own restaurant, tennis court and swimming pool. Anyone who prefers living in a tent or a caravan should make for one of the up-market campsites nearby which provide a whole range of facilities but may well be crowded at the height of the season.

**Matalascañas**, which marks the end of the coast road, is larger,
noisier, and apparently determined to outdo the Costa del Sol. It is
completely tourist orientated with everything from riding stables,
which are open all the year round, to discotheques and other carefully planned entertainments that last far into the night. The hotels
are entirely predictable. The best, and therefore the most sought
after, caters for everyone and also for most sporting interests apart,
at the moment, from golf. It is an ideal centre for all types of water
sports and outdoor activities, particularly sailing and windsurfing,
but its celebrations tend to be popular rather than traditional.

With nothing further to the east except deserted beaches which
give way almost immediately to the sand dunes and marshes of the
Guadalquivir delta, there is literally nowhere to go from
Matalascañas except back to Tore de la Higuera, almost on the
outskirts. Here a turning leads northwards through El Rocío to
Almonte, past the famous **Parque Nacional de Doñana**. The park
provides a haven for migrating birds and a home for many local
species as well as a whole host of reptiles, fish and a variety of
different animals. Specially conducted tours, using Land Rovers, set
out from the Casa Control, off the road to El Rocío. Details of these
organised visits are obtainable from the tourist offices in Huelva and
Sevilla but they may not include a warning to take along a large bottle
of insect repellent — the region is also extremely popular with
mosquitoes!

The tiny village of **El Rocío** has little of interest. It would probably
never be noticed if it were not for the famous Whitsun pilgrimage,
certainly the largest and probably the oldest in Spain. According to
legend the whole thing started in the thirteenth century when a local
shepherd discovered a statue of the Virgin in a hollow tree. He
decided to take it to Almonte but when he woke up from his
afternoon siesta he found that the little carved figure had made her
own way back to the tree. A hermitage was promptly built on the
spot to give the statue a more substantial home and within no time
it became a place of pilgrimage. Over the centuries more and more
people converged on El Rocío to pay their respects to the Virgin of the
Marshes and until today the crowd is numbered at about one million.

The pilgrimage gets under way the week before Whitsun. The
Brotherhoods most closely connected with the celebrations are accompanied by several thousand people on horseback, on foot and in
covered wagons decorated with flowers. At night they gather round
camp fires and when they reach El Rocío the pilgrims are joined by
hordes of onlookers who time their arrival to coincide with the

procession of Brotherhoods as they wind their way to the church to pay homage to the Virgin.

**Almonte**, which is responsible for the Coto de Doñana, the El Rocío sanctuary and the Matalascañas beach, is only a short drive to the north. It is an administrative centre, dating for the most part from the eighteenth century, with a healthy bank account and not a great deal in the way of memorable buildings. Nevertheless it makes a good base from which to explore the interior of the province as there are one or two perfectly acceptable hotels and several different roads to choose from, including one to Sevilla. Its nearest neighbours south of the Huelva-Sevilla highway are Rociana del Condado and Bollullos par del Condado, both surrounded by strawberry beds and by vineyards that are said to have produced the wine chosen by the Conquistadores to take with them across the Atlantic. There are connections with both the highway and the major road that runs parallel to it, the latter being through La Palma del Condado which boasts two convents, a fifteenth-century hermitage and a parish church that is a typical example of Andalucían Baroque.

Once north of the highway there is little doubt that **Niebla** has more in the way of historic attractions than anywhere else. There is nothing tangible to connect it with the mythological splendour of *Tartessus* or the Celtic town of *Ilipla* but the Roman bridge is still very much in existance. The walls, built by the Arabs, are anything up to 15m (50ft) thick and pierced by four gateways known respectively as del Agua, del Buey, del Sevilla and del Socorro. They rest on foundations laid down by the Romans on the banks of the Río Tinto. Tucked away inside are the remains of an old Mozarab temple that was transformed into a mosque before being converted to Christianity after the town was recaptured in 1257. There are several attractive little villages dotted about the fertile countryside, among them Trigueros which has a fine parish church and keeps an eye on the almost perfectly preserved Dolmen del Soto.

Further north still, east of the highway to Extremadura, is **Valverde del Camino**, an extremely busy little town which is better known for its craftsmanship than for its architecture. It is one of the best places to buy leather boots and shoes, copperware and wooden articles of various descriptions. A road of no outstanding merit links the village with **Nerva**, birthplace of the painter Vázquez Días and centre of the mining area. Anyone with an eye for the unusual would be well advised to take a quick look at the enormous open cast Río Tinto Mines, some of which have been in operation for well over 2,000 years. They are both spectacular and colourful, surrounded by hills rich in pyrites, copper, silver and gold. The town itself has little of interest to offer the visitor apart from some English-type houses and the knowledge that it was probably the first place in Spain to stage a football match after the game was introduced by mining personnel in the nineteenth century.

The Sierra de Aracena, in the north of Huelva, is one of the greenest and loveliest areas in Andalucía. The rolling foothills of the Sierra Morena are doused in oaks, walnut trees and chestnuts which are a blaze of colour in the autumn. The main town is **Aracena**, rising in steps up the hillside and overlooked by the ruins of a Moorish castle that was once the property of the Knights Templar. Apart from their original church with its eye-catching doorway and Mudéjar tower, faintly reminiscent of the Giralda Tower in Sevilla, there are a clutch of ancient churches, a sixteenth-century hermitage and an elderly synagogue. The local hotels are adequate without being in any way memorable and are augmented by one or two small restaurants in the vicinity of the **Gruta de las Maravillas**.

These caves are by no means a recent discovery although the grottoes were flooded until it was decided to drain them nearly a hundred years ago. The complex consists of a dozen or so different caverns, long galleries and a series of limpid pools, all hollowed out by underground rivers running underneath the castle walls. They are filled with rainbow coloured rock formations resembling pillars, draperies and outcrops of coral as well as sparkling white crystals that give their name to the Well of Snows. Conducted tours are arranged each morning and afternoon and last for about an hour. An added attraction is the newly created open-air museum of contemporary art while souvenir hunters spend their time selecting representative items made by the local potters and hand embroidered articles which are another feature of the region.

There are several places of interest in the vicinity of Aracena. **Zufre**, for example, has a distinctly Moorish atmosphere, a number of aged houses and a parish church with an altarpiece said to be the work of Alonso Cano. On the other hand **Alájar**, on the edge of an area well known for its cherry and apple orchards, is justly proud of the natural caves of Sillita del Rey and the Salón de los Machos and its traditional pilgrimage of the Queen of Angels in September.

The northernmost place of interest west of the Extremadura-Huelva highway is **Encinasola**, only a stone's throw from the border. It has managed to preserve the remains of a Moorish castle, some medieval towers and a selection of eighteenth-century buildings besides occupying its time making traditional rugs. Nevertheless the village attracts fewer tourists than **Aroche**, to the south, which makes a determined effort to attract as many visitors as possible. It has turned its ancient castle into a bullring, restored several of the older houses and opened two museums, one of which is devoted to archaeology. Numbered among its other attractions are a lively annual carnival and a rather more sedate Whitsun pilgrimage.

**Cortegana**, on the road back to the main highway, contents itself with the Megalithic burial ground of Los Llanos de la Belleza, part of an old Roman road, a crumbling fortress and two somewhat updated churches, not to mention its busy local potteries. From here a minor road sets off through the attractive countryside to **Almonaster la Real** where the castle contains the remnants of a mosque built during the great days of the Moorish occupation. Given the necessary time and inclination it is worth wandering through the narrow streets with their Mudéjar and Gothic houses and pausing to inspect the Door of Forgiveness at the local parish church. There are also a couple of small but quite forgettable hotels where it is possible to find a bed for the night.

Back on the southbound highway **Calañas** has even less to offer in the way of accommodation but is a good jumping off place for **Puebla de Guzmán**, much of which dates from the eighteenth century. It is remarkable mainly for the spring festival in honour of the Virgin Mary when many of the women wear their traditional costumes. **Alosno** is much more interested in music, which is hardly surprising because it is said to be the home of the fandango and entertains itself and its visitors with a variation which it insists is infinitely more authentic than anything on offer elsewhere. During the Feast of San Juan, which coincides with the summer solstice and is therefore believed to have strong pagan undertones, dancers equipped with little bells take part in the procession down the attractive Calle Real before giving a spirited performance inside the seventeenth-century parish church. Sticks and bells are also much in evidence during the Crosses of May festivities while Christmas time is marked by the La Rama pilgrimage.

Huelva province celebrates as often and as enthusiastically as anywhere else in Andalucía. The capital gives each New Year a rousing send-off with the Cavalcade of the Three Kings on 5 January, followed 15 days later by fiestas in a whole host of towns and villages in honour of San Sebastián, the patron saint of Huelva. Holy Week and Corpus Christi are marked by solemn processions while the Fiestas del Carmen on 16 July attract ever increasing crowds to the coastal resorts. The Fiestas Colombinas on 3 August recall the epic voyage of discovery and, although always very colourful, took on an added dimension in 1992, marking the passage of five centuries in the history of Spain and its one-time possessions in the New World.

# 7
# *JAÉN*

---

J aén, one of the two most northerly provinces of Andalucía, is a
delightful region which deserves to be far better known and much
more frequently visited. Scenically, historically and architecturally it
has a great deal to offer the visitor. Facilities are available for a wide
range of sports including hunting and fishing, there are some comfortable hotels, a number of campsites, typical local dishes that vary
from one area to another and a variety of fairs and festivals.

The province — known as the Silver Gate of Andalucía — is
completely landlocked with Córdoba to the west, Granada in the
south, Albacete on the far side of the eastern Segura and Cazorla
mountains and the Sierra Morena separating it from Ciudad Real
and the rest of Northern Spain. Gradually the countryside begins to
level out, giving way to hills covered with a patchwork quilt of olive
groves said to produce some of the finest fruit and oil to be found. The
western plains under extensive fields of wheat are edged in places
with modest vineyards that merge in with the olive trees, whereas
the mining areas to the north consist of scrubland interspersed with
sunflowers and pastures where fighting bulls are raised.

The whole of Jaén is peppered with ancient castles, extremely
attractive little towns and villages and the sites of battles fought there
long ago. Just how long ago depends on which area is under
discussion. In some places it was a Carthaginian skirmish or a
Roman fracas with the local inhabitants, in others a Moorish take-
over, a Christian victory or even a French defeat which changed the
whole course of the Spanish War of Independence. The churches
range from large, ornate constructions to famous isolated sanctuaries while a dozen or so different museums concern themselves with
everything from archaeology to what are rather oddly described as
'Popular Manners'. There is practically nothing left over in the region

from prehistoric times, and very little building work to connect it with the Romans or the Visigoths but from the early days of the Moorish occupation onwards it has much of interest.

**Jaén**, the provincial capital and known to the Moors as *Geen* (the way of caravans) is not a particularly large or overbearing centre, which is definitely an advantage where visitors are concerned. It is situated in the south-west at the foot of the Sierra de Jabalcuz, surrounded by olive trees, with several highrise buildings in the modern sector and a giant cathedral completely dominating the old part of the town. This began life in 1500 on the site of an ancient mosque and took the best part of 200 years to complete. Its chief architect was Andrés de Vandelvira who, although the façade is considered to be his masterpiece, is said by some critics to have rather over-reached himself. There was simply not enough space available to do justice to his grandiose ideas. After his death in 1576 there was apparently no-one who would, or perhaps could, scale down his plans to fit into their somewhat cramped surroundings. The result is that it is impossible to see more than a small section of the building from any given vantage point unless one takes to the air.

The façade is remarkably impressive. Eight tall, decorative columns, interspersed with statues and reliefs, support an open balustrade on which stand the figures of St Ferdinand, the Evangelists and other religious dignitaries flanked by two vast square towers, each rounded off with a matching dome.

There are three soaring naves, an ornate choir and a chapel behind the high altar containing the Santo Rosto reliquary. Also in the chapel is the ancient Virgen de la Antigua who, according to legend, went into battle with St Ferdinand and was largely responsible for the success of his campaigns. In addition to the many sculptures and paintings to be seen in the body of the church quantities of other treasures are housed below ground in the Cathedral Museum.

The city also has an enviable collection of smaller churches and monasteries. The fortress-church of San Ildefonso, with some well-preserved carvings, is some three blocks to the east of the cathedral but most of the others are strung out in a companionable fashion on the opposite side of the old town. The nearest, but quite a walk away, is the Santa Clara Monastery, founded in the thirteenth century. The Capilla San Andrés, also known as the Chapel of the Immaculate Conception, dates back to the sixteenth century.

Apart from La Magdalena, the oldest church of all, which replaced an ancient mosque, the other main attractions within strolling distance are the Arch of San Lorenzo and the extensive Arab baths. These are also known as Ali's Bathing Houses after the eleventh-

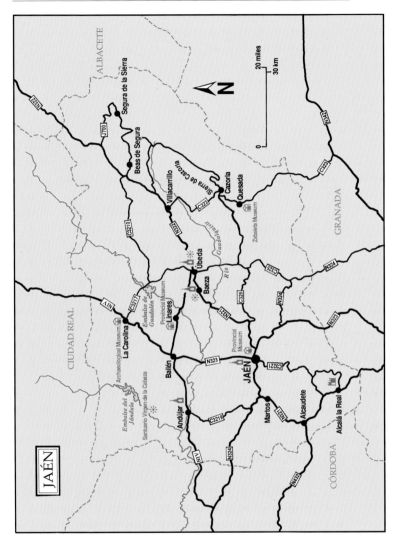

century Moorish king of Jaén and are claimed to be among the largest and most important of their kind in Spain. Finally, stretched out along a mountaintop about 4km (2 miles) to the west of the capital, is the gigantic castle-fortress of Santa Catalina, now home to an up-market *parador*. It has been tastefully restored so as not to damage either the fabric or the atmosphere, enhanced by tapestries, period furniture, pictures and objects d'art. There is vaulting which would not look out of place in a cathedral, and magnificent views from the castle walls.

Far below, in the city centre, are half a dozen listed hotels and hostels as well as restaurants and bars, cinemas and discos, swimming pools, football grounds, horses and an interesting provincial museum. Jaén also has a small aerodrome but uses the airports at Granada and Córdoba, both about 100km (62 miles) away. There are also regular train services, buses to other provincial centres including Madrid, Barcelona, Benidorm, Granada and Sevilla and plenty of taxis. The banks are open from 9am to 2pm whereas the shops and department stores take a 3-hour lunch break at 1.30pm but do not close again until 7.30pm or 8pm, depending on the time of year. There are main roads to Madrid, Córdoba, and Granada, a slightly roundabout route to Málaga and direct links with Murcia and Almería. An interwoven pattern of secondary roads, usually in good condition, connects all the main places of interest, leaving a host of small byways to take care of the outlying hamlets and beauty spots.

There are not a great many places of interest to the south-west of the capital. **Martos**, 23km (14 miles) distant, insists that it is the largest olive growing centre in Spain. It is a small, off-white town built on the hillside below Peña Castle with a parish church of no great moment, a collection of tombstones, coins and other items associated with the Romans and an industrial section concerned almost entirely with olives. Meanwhile Alcaudete, slightly further down the road, is overshadowed by its Moorish castle and is extremely proud of the Church of Santa María.

**Alcalá la Real** has rather more to boast about. The impressive castle of La Mota commands a magnificent view of the surrounding countryside with its chequerboard of olive groves. Not far away is a much smaller but equally severe old Homage Tower. The town, known as *Al-Kalaat Be Zayde* in Moorish times, was the birthplace of the sculptor Juan Martinez Montañés who produced some very emotive work before he died in 1649 at the age of 80. There are some attractive, partly restored mansions, the Church of Santa María la Mayor and an elderly town hall but nothing worth mentioning in the way of hotels or restaurants.

The main road to Madrid follows the Río Guadalbullón northwards almost to **Bailén** where there is a *parador* complete with swimming pool, a selection of smaller establishments and a most acceptable motel. The town itself is entirely forgettable except for the fact that it gave its name to an important battle which resulted in the overwhelming defeat of Napoleon's forces in 1808. The anniversary is celebrated with great enthusiasm and much merrymaking from the 18 to the 22 July every year. A short distance away, on the far side of a small campsite, is **Baños de la Encina** which was also involved in the fighting. It is a neat, quite well-ordered town, surrounded by farmlands and olive groves and dominated by a large church and an even larger fortress built by Al-Hakam II in 967.

**Andújar**, on the road from Bailén to Córdoba, is the chief town of  the area, ideally situated on the banks of the Guadalquivir. It is a most attractive, if industrial, centre full of houses and little chapels which have survived almost intact since the fifteenth and sixteenth centuries. The Roman bridge with its fourteen arches is one of the main tourist attractions, along with a small motor museum and the town's  individual pottery. The Church of San Miguel in the Plaza de España is worth seeing for its massive carved wood door, the statues of the prophets and a fine wrought iron grille. The Church of Santa María, which is only open to visitors from early April to the end of October, has an even more eye-catching grille, El Greco's painting *Christ in the Garden of Olives* and Pacheco's *Assumption of the Virgin*. Not to be totally outdone the severe white church of San Bartolomé relies for its effect on a beautifully carved sixteenth-century door. The town boasts a couple of modest hotels and a well-equipped campsite on the Madrid-Cádiz highway which is open all through the year. Alternatively, the small spa town of **Marmolejo**, 10km (6 miles) down the road, is famous for making guitars and has a perfectly acceptable hotel with a restaurant and a swimming pool.

A minor but quite busy road heads up into the **Sierra Morena** to pay its respects to the Virgen de la Cabeza. As usual there is a legend attached to this isolated mountain sanctuary. It is said that in 1227 a one-armed shepherd had a vision in which he was told that his arm would be restored if a chapel was built on a lonely rock in the vicinity. Both sides of the bargain were duly honoured, the chapel was later replaced by a monastery and the spot became a well-known place of pilgrimage. In September 1936 well over 200 Civil Guards, ardent Nationalists and some of the local townspeople took refuge in the area. Despite everything the Republicans could throw against them they managed to hold out for about 8 months but when eventually they surrendered the Virgin and all the buildings had literally gone up in smoke. Restoration work was undertaken as quickly as possible, a new statue was installed and now, on the last weekend in April, thousands of people converge on the site in decorated carts and cavalcades of motor cars and buses including members of the Brotherhoods and their attendant pilgrims, whose attention is fixed

*The façade of Jaén Cathedral*

*Pottery souvenirs on the road to La Carolina*

on the Virgin in her red and gold robes. The town of Andújar joins in the celebrations as well as holding a special fair on 8-12 September.

To the north-east of Bailén, on the Madrid highway, the town of **La Carolina** is a comparative newcomer to the scene, mainly industrial and rather uninteresting as far as tourists are concerned, although it does have an archaeological museum and one acceptable hotel. On  the other hand the route is peppered with wayside inns and restaurants, low buildings crouching behind mounds of pots and other souvenirs as well as wire screens covered with decorative plates.

At **Las Navas de Tolosa**, which suffered badly at the hands of the Moors and the Christians in their vicious struggles for supremacy, there is a small hostel with facilities for both tennis and swimming. Nearby Santa Elena, another ancient trouble spot, has a campsite with all the necessary amenities which is open from May to the end of September. Either would make a possible base for exploring the Despeñaperros Pass, now, as in the olden days, a natural gateway to the north. It was here, in 1212, that a shepherd guided the Christian armies along a little known track through the mountains, thereby enabling them to take the Almohad forces by surprise and prepare the way for the reconquest of Andalucía. More recently it was bandit country, inhabited largely by wolves and criminals, where even the most carefree traveller would think twice before deviating from the road. In this day and age the only hunting allowed is for certain varieties of small game — any remaining wolves are a protected species and must not on any account be either captured or killed.

There are several reservoirs in the north of Jaén province, among them the Embalse del Jándula, where there is swimming and a certain amount of river fishing, and the Embalse de Guadalén to the north-east of Linares. The whole area is essentially mining country, a stark, arid, semi-wasteland blanketed over with low, dry scrub. **Linares** is the largest town in Jaén apart from the capital but has little or nothing to attract the visitor apart from an interesting archaeological section attached to the provincial museum. This contains a great  many items discovered in the vicinity, especially in the ruins of Castulo, the ancient capital of Spain. The town takes itself very seriously, even to the extent of holding an International Chess Competition every year in March, followed by the Fair of St Augustine during the last week of August.

To the south-east of Linares, along what is described as the Renaissance Route, a series of little villages vie for attention. Ibros offers some elderly ramparts, Sabiote an old villa and Canena a little spa, but the two most oustanding towns are, without question, Baeza and Úbeda, both of which are rated as historic monuments.

In its early days **Baeza** was an important Moorish frontier post and the first town to be captured by the Christians in 1227, after which it played an important role in the reconquest of Andalucía. It is literally crammed with splendid old buildings, occasional squares and fountains, and some quite spectacular ruins. The first place to make for, partly because it is the home of the local tourist office, is the Plaza de los Leones. The square takes its name from a small fountain, unearthed in Castulo and guarded by four unlikely looking lions whose features have been sadly eroded by time and the elements.

❋ The most eye-catching approach is through the Jaén Gate, an archway constructed in the original walls in the early sixteenth century in honour of the Emperor Charles V who looked in briefly in 1526 en route for Sevilla and his marriage to Isabel of Portugal. At right-angles to the arch, the Casa del Pópulo was the former law courts with six matching doors opening out from the offices of the appropriate notaries but occupied these days by the tourist office. The hearings took place in the courtroom on the first floor, linked to the archway by a rounded balcony. Facing the Jaén Gate, the one-time abattoir is an imposing structure complete with a covered balcony, heavy grilles over the windows and a large imperial coat-of-arms. It was built around 1540 but considerably restored in 1962.

Å A small pedestrian walkway, interrupted by a pleasing little square, pushes past several elderly houses to the Plaza Santa María, overlooked by the cathedral from the top of a wide flight of steps. The present building dates from the thirteenth century, when it replaced an ancient mosque, but it was considerably altered and up-dated by Vandelvira 300 years later. Adjoining the cathedral, and also facing the square, is the Casa Consistoriales Altas, decorated with the coats-of-arms of Juana the Mad and her husband Philip the Fair. On the third side, opposite the cathedral, is the seventeenth-century seminary. The walls are covered in graffiti due to the students' time honoured custom of writing their names and the dates on which they graduated in bull's blood wherever they could find an empty space. The centrepiece of this sloping, cobble-encrusted plaza is the Santa María Fountain, a small but decorative triumphal arch standing in a shallow basin roughly the shape of a four-leaf clover.

🏛 Down a narrow street, a few steps away, the Palace of Los Marqueses de Jabalquinto is a most desirable residence in the Isabeline style. The large interior courtyard behind heavy, studded doors, looks unusually deserted at the moment except for two stone lions guarding an impressive Baroque staircase on the far side. The whole building is in the process of being renovated and restored but it should be well worth seeing when the work is completed. Opposite the palace the very under-stated Church of Santa Cruz is the only survivor from the thirteenth century when the Christians celebrated their occupation of the town by replacing all the Arab mosques with churches of their own.

By the middle of the sixteenth century Baeza was a cultural centre  as well as a beautiful town. The ancient university, just round the corner from the Jabalquinto palace, was built at about this time and continued to accept students for nearly 300 years. Nowadays its pupils are all school children but, even so, visitors are allowed in to the large patio and shown the beautiful Mudéjar ceiling in the main hall. Other buildings of interest include the former Corn Exchange next door, the town hall which started life as a prison, the Casa de Comedias and the Montemar Palace, once the home of the Counts of Garcíez. Foremost among the clutch of small churches is San Andrés with its collection of Gothic paintings housed in the sacristy. Finally, it would be a pity to miss the distinctive ruins of the Church of San Francisco which was obviously another Vandelvira masterpiece. The greater part of it has disappeared, leaving the remains of the transept and some stone altarpieces open to both passersby and to the weather. For the visitor who feels inclined to linger in this medieval atmosphere there is a modest hotel on the Arca del Aqua Avenue and a couple of smaller places quite close by.

Roughly 10km (6 miles) to the east of Baeza, along a well maintained road through the olive groves, is the equally fascinating but somewhat larger town of **Úbeda**, once described as the Salamanca of Andalucía. During the Moorish occupation it was known as *Ubbadat-al-Arab* but when the Christians finally took possession in 1234 this was abbreciated quite considerably. There is not much to see on the outskirts, and some of the little narrow streets can be ignored, but that leaves a formidable list of places that should not be missed.

The most beautiful square is undoubtedly the Plaza Vázquez de  Molina with its splendid array of ancient buildings including the imposing Church of El Salvador, designed by Diego de Siloé with a little help from Vandelvira who was responsible for the sacristy. The  façade with its coats-of arms, statues and other carvings is attractively ornate but gives little indication of the extravagant and frankly over decorated interior with its monumental iron screen and massive eighteenth-century altarpiece. El Salvador was built for Francisco de los Cobos, who was Secretary of State at the time of Charles V, spent most of his considerable fortune making Ubeda more beautiful and is buried in the church. The courtyard outside is shared by the Condestable Dávalos Palace, a large sixteenth-century mansion that belonged to Dean Ortega and has now been converted into a *parador*. It is worth a visit, even if you do not happen to be staying there, because of its original ceilings, lovely open fireplaces and extremely good restaurant.

Separated from the *parador* by a narrow street, the Casa de las Cadenas takes its name from the chains surrounding the forecourt. It was designed by Vandelvira in 1562 and is currently home to both the town hall and the tourist office. The most decorative side looks out on to the Plaza Vázquez de Molina across a small, well-manicured garden and a very restrained six-sided fountain, although the main entrance is in the Plaza del Ayuntamiento round the corner. Apart from an arcaded patio it keeps some mural paintings from the former chapterhouse on the first floor which can be inspected almost any morning by request.

Several other buildings contribute to the general atmosphere of this exceptionally beautiful square. The solid corner tower of the sixteenth-century palace of the Marquéz de Mancera, a one-time Viceroy of Peru, has an uninterrupted view across the cobblestones to the Church of Santa María de los Reales Alcázares. The main things to see inside are the chapels with their wrought iron grilles, largely the work of Master Bartolomé, and the seventeenth-century cloister. Also facing the square are the Old Jail of the Bishop and the equally antiquated Posito, built in the style which has been popular ever since Úbeda was recaptured from the Moors.

There are places of interest at frequent intervals in the cobweb of little streets surrounding the Plaza Vázquez de Molina, although by no means all of them are open to the public. On the far side of the Casa de las Cadenas, near the Corazón de Jesús, are the 200-year-old Contadero Mansion, the profusely decorated Casa de las Torres and the Church of Santo Domingo whose south door, handsomely carved with scrolls and roses, opens out on to an attractive little square. A few blocks away, on the Cava Rastro, stone soldiers carrying coats-of-arms guard the entrance to the La Rambla Palace, whereas the Casa de los Salvajes takes its name from two figures dressed in animal skins held together at the waist by belts apparently cut from the tendrils of blackberry bushes. The Plaza Primero de Mayo is worth a visit, partly on account of the fourteenth-century Rosebush Gate and partly in order to see the Church of San Pablo, built in the early 1500s. Its main features are an impressive entrance, the richly carved Mercedes Chapel and the Heads of the Dead Chapel, the latter bearing all the hallmarks of Andrés de Vandelvira.

There are a couple of other palatial mansions in the immediate vicinity but anyone reacting against a surfeit of medieval architecture would be well advised to head for the Calle Valencia, no great distance away beyond the ancient walls. It is by far the best place to look for pottery, much of which is deep green in colour and beauti-

*St James Matamore over the entrance to the Hospital de Santiago, Úbeda*

fully glazed. Alternatively, visitors with a sense of humour might prefer the Plaza de Andalucía at the other end of the Calle Real. The ✳ square itself is nothing much to write home about but the fountain in the middle has a telling reminder of the comparatively recent Civil War. The metal statue reflected in the water is a likeness of General Sero whose Fascist affiliations did not go down at all well with the people of the town. At the first opportunity a number of local marksmen peppered it with bullets, one of them scoring a direct hit to the head, after which the somewhat draughty general was left as a warning to anyone else who might be tempted to share his ideas.

At the opposite end of the Obispo Cobos, adjacent to the bullring, is the sixteenth-century Hospital de Santiago which has been described as the Escorial of Andalucía. It has a splendid high relief of St James Matamore, several smaller figures and two saintly statues at roof level, an arcaded patio, a grand staircase and a large quadrangle that makes an ideal playground for school children who look on it as a private football pitch.

Apart from the *parador,* Úbeda has a few other modest hotels, a smattering of totally forgettable bars and little restaurants and a taxi rank in the Plaza de Andalucía. There is nothing remarkable about its local museum, in fact the tourist maps do not even mention it, and there is some confusion about its opening hours. Nor, apparently, does the town have much time for festivals although it does celebrate Holy Week in style and lets its hair down for several days at the end of September when everyone goes to St Michael's Fair.

The area to the south of Baeza and Úbeda is rather short of tourist attractions apart from **Jimena**, an off-white town which has some not very spectacular Neolithic paintings in the Cueva de la Grantja and a reasonably pleasant church. However, a choice of small roads thread their way across country to **Cazorla** and the mountainous region all round. It is an attractive, well organised little centre, part of which clambers up the hillside towards the ruined Arab castle of La Yedra. Some of the alleys are less like streets than stairways, but there are two large squares, a number of old houses and elderly convents as well as the ruined church of Santa María. Augmenting Cazorla's collection of modest hotels is the isolated Parador El Adelantado, a tidy drive away along a road that meanders through the pine forests. There is nothing historic about this comparatively small white building, better described as a hunting lodge, geared to guests interested in walking, fishing, shooting or sightseeing.

Among the clutch of small places within easy reach of Cazorla is **Peal del Becerro** where the local church is of less moment than the Iberian sepulchral chamber of Toya quite close by. The Sanctuary of Tiscar to the south is sited at the entrance to an impressive pass and is the home of the local Virgin, at least for part of the year. On the first Sunday in May she is escorted with due pomp and ceremony to the town of Quesada to spend a holiday in semi-urban surroundings before returning home in a similar fashion at the beginning of September. **Quesada** is another mountain eyrie, poised above a gorge and surrounded by dragon's tooth crags and man-made terraces dotted here and there with small white houses. Like Cazorla it has collected enough artifacts to set up a small museum which in this case is filled mainly with the paintings of Rafael Zabaleta.

Anyone choosing an alternative route to the north-east would probably opt for the main road from Úbeda to Albacete. It calls first at **Villacarrillo**, an unremarkable town known principally for its Church of the Assumption and the enjoyment it gets out of bull-running through the narrow streets in the manner made famous by Pamplona, in the north of Spain. A short distance away there is a turning off through Beas de Segura, surrounded by olives with a convent that reserves a place in its chapel for Santa Teresa de Jesus, to the village of Hornos at the tip of the Tranco Dam, so far one of the largest in the country. Determined efforts are being made to turn the whole area into a holiday resort and already there is a small

Guadalmena sailing club and facilities for a variety of water sports.

**Segura de la Sierra**, to the north-east, is an extremely photogenic  hilltop town where the Phoenicians and the Romans are believed to have kept everyone busy mining iron and silver before the Visigoths moved in. They, in turn, were given their marching orders by the Moors who converted it into a frontier post on the outskirts of Andalucía and built a typical fortress which, unfortunately, has been rather too enthusiastically restored. The scattered villages of Ocera with its little sixteenth-century church, Siles, Benatal and Genave are all earmarked for development with tourists in mind and make much of their various festivals during the second half of the year.

Regardless of all its man-made attractions, visitors who visit the **Sierra de Cazorla y Segura** are usually much more interested in the scenery and the nature reserve than in obscure castles and miniscule  museums. Much of the area is uninhabited, several of the minor roads are hardly more than cart tracks and occasionally one of them loses both heart and its sense of direction and gives up the unequal struggle. But it is a magnificent place for walking, especially in the  forest areas of the Sierra de Cazorla where there are marked footpaths with maps available from the National Institute for the Conservation of Nature (ICONA) or from the national tourist offices.

The Río Guadalquivir starts out as a spring in La Cañada de las Fuentes, a glen at the foot of the Arroyo de Santo Domingo, not far from Quesada. Fishing in this region is excellent, especially for trout in the Borosa and Río Guadalentin or barbel, bream and pike in the Guadalquivir. At one time hunting was popular but this is now also carefully controlled. Licences are available, subject to various conditions such as the categories of game, the type of guns and the seasons determined each year by the Ministry for Agriculture.

People who have no interest in either shooting or fishing will find a great many other things on which to focus their attention. For example, it is said that there are species of wild flowers and butterflies that cannot be duplicated anywhere else in the world, although it requires a certain knowledge and determination to identify them. Also there is no closed season where photographers are concerned.

Sightseeing apart, it is useful to know something about the weather in Jaén. The province is included in the dry lands of Spain although there is a certain amount of rain up in the mountains. The summers are hot, but it is as well to take something warm because the evenings along the Guadalquivir Valley can turn decidedly cool whereas the winters are cold and fairly miserable. Most local menus are traditional rather than sophisticated, using seasonal ingredients produced in the area concerned.

# 8
# *MÁLAGA*

Málaga is the smallest province in Andalucía but it is also the most heavily encrusted with tourists, ex-patriots from many different countries, tall concrete buildings, hypermarkets, golf courses, buses and building materials. However, once away from the narrow coastal belt it also has some of the most impressive dolmens to be found anywhere, ruined Roman settlements, well preserved Moorish castles, Christian palaces and atmospheric little villages. There are enough hills to underline the claim that Spain is the most mountainous country in Europe apart from Switzerland, as well as man-made lakes, valleys fragrant with orange and lemon blossom and fields of sunflowers interspersed with rare Spanish firs, mimosa and almond trees.

Apart from its lengthy coastline Málaga is bordered by Cádiz, Sevilla and Granada with just a few kilometres of Córdoba up in the north-east. The province can be divided roughly into five different sections. The Sierra de Ronda consists of a number of small mountain ranges grouped around a central plateau and covered with low scrub, oak trees and Spanish firs. This gives way to the Antequera basin which is reasonably fertile and sprinkled with small lagoons providing a natural habitat for various species of migratory birds including flamingos. The Axarquia region in the south-east is a study in contrasts — high, isolated areas, until quite recently the haunt of bandits, which see few visitors, whereas the shoreline is seldom, if ever, free of them. At the same time the so-called Vélez Valley still produces the identical top quality fruit that was being exported to the Middle East more than a thousand years ago. The capital and the area surrounding it is cosmopolitan and crowded although most of its visitors are usually in transit, making for one of the thriving tourist resorts further down the coast.

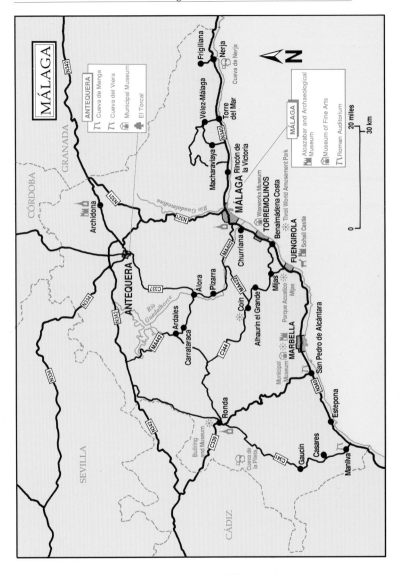

The region is rich in history, starting with Bronze Age man, whose relics have been discovered in the province. The Phoenicians established a trading post they called *Malaka*, leaving the Greeks to found

*Mainake* in about 600BC, probably in the area of Torre del Mar, which was destroyed by the Carthaginians after the battle of Alalia when it was less than 100 years old. Then came the Romans who stayed long enough to build settlements of their own, complete with theatres, temples, villas and public baths that were promptly obliterated by the Byzantines and the Visigoths who conquered Málaga in 570. The Moors arrived next and remained for more than 700 years until they were driven out by the Catholic Monarchs at the end of the fifteenth century. Like the rest of Andalucía, Málaga immediately went into a decline from which it only started to recover about 300 years later. By the middle of the nineteenth century the city had become industrialised with sugar refineries, shipyards and textile mills, but it was not until tourists began to arrive a quarter of a century ago that Málaga became both well known and affluent.

The roads in Málaga vary from good to sometimes quite unpleasant. The recently completed motorways linking the city with both Sevilla and Granada and along the coast from Rincón de la Victoria to Algeciras are excellent. The latter has helped to reduce the amount of traffic using the highway which hugs the shores of the Mediterranean from one end of the province to the other. Previously motorists would go out of their way to avoid it but the many improvements, such as central barriers, have helped considerably. In addition there is an excellent road slicing into the hillsides up to Ronda from San Pedro de Alcántara that carries on to join the highway linking Antequera with Jerez, while another similar route heads northwards to Córdoba. Many of the secondary roads are in reasonably good condition although it is advisable to keep a constant lookout for unexpected potholes and damaged verges. Byways can be astonishingly good or absolutely frightful, changing from one to the other without warning.

There is accommodation in Málaga to fit all pockets, although there may be a shortage at the height of the season. There are *paradores* in the capital, Nerja, Antequera and Torremolinos, plenty of five and four star hotels on or near the coast and many other lower grade establishments. Most towns of any size have furnished villas and apartments to let and there are campsites at regular intervals along the coast but hardly any acceptable ones further inland.

Restaurants are just as easy to come by, and as varied. There are Chinese, Italian, Scandinavian but strangely not many Indian restaurants, many others that specialise in seafood and dozens more run by British ex-patriots. For anyone who is anxious to try the local dishes the Spanish themselves offer a variety of traditional menus. *Ajo blanco* is a cold soup made from almonds and garlic and served with a few grapes floating on top whereas its hot counterpart, *cachorrenas*, consists largely of bitter orange and salt cod. *Rape a la malaguena* is angler fish baked in a casserole with onions, almonds, tomatoes and seasoning, swordfish is equally good hot or cold while for sheer novelty there is nothing to beat fresh sardines and anchovies skewered and cooked over hot coals on the beach. Pork is served everywhere, in dishes like *lomo al moscatel* when it is baked with wine and cinnamon, veal is the main ingredient in a stew called *choto* whereas *chivo frito* is fried kid. Many sweets and cakes were introduced originally by the Arabs and are still made in several convents by nuns using ancient recipes.

For sports enthusiasts there are first class golf courses, riding stables, tennis courts, yacht marinas with charter facilities and equipment for hire, as well as swimming pools and facilities for windsurfing, water parachuting and underwater fishing. Less energetic holidaymakers can find a large amusement park, an aquatic centre and a zoo, in addition to bullfighting and stock car racing in the Mijas area. Evening entertainments range from cinemas, theatres and casinos to flamenco shows, discos and even bingo. Every month has its special festivals, starting with the Cavalcade of the Three Kings in January, followed by Carnival, Holy Week processions leading up to Easter and festivals in honour of many patron saints. There is a pagan feast marking the summer solstice, a ritual sardine funeral, cattle fairs, concerts and the famous Verdailes, or folk music festival, in the hills above the capital on 28 December.

Although **Málaga** city may not be everyone's idea of an ideal holiday resort it has managed to preserve a good deal of the past while, at the same time, expanding rapidly. The Alcazaba, built by the Moors in the ninth century on a hilltop site chosen originally by the Phoenicians was updated by the Romans when they occupied Andalucía. Unfortunately it is showing its age rather badly and now consists of little more than a series of ancient fortified walls and towers enclosing attractive, terraced gardens leading up to the city's Archaeological Museum. Just outside the ramparts are the remains of a Roman auditorium, built in the second century AD and now used during the summer for Málaga's International Theatre Festival. A walkway leads up to the Gibralfaro Castle at the top of the hill, which may have replaced an ancient lighthouse, with the *parador* nearby.

Next in order of seniority is the cathedral which replaced an Arab mosque in the late sixteenth century. Work on the building stopped before the second tower was completed, hence its local name of La Manquita, or The One-armed Woman. A short walk away, in the

Tapas *bars, like this one at Torremolinos, are popular for quick snacks*

Plaza de la Merced, the birthplace of Pablo Picasso is being fully restored as a museum of his life and work. Also in the same area is the Museum of Fine Arts, housed in an ancient palace. The Museo de Semana Santa is the place to see splendid thrones and statues associated with Holy Week, whereas a seventeenth-century inn on the Avenida de la Rosaleda, running along the side of the Río Guadalmedia, makes an appropriate setting for the Museum of Popular Art.

Málaga also has its fair share of churches. El Sagrario, in the shadow of the cathedral, was originally a mosque transformed by the addition of a high altar in the sixteenth century while, at the same time, the Church of Santiago managed to retain its Moorish tower. The city hall, built at the beginning of this century in the Spanish Renaissance style, is surrounded by gardens containing some quite unusual trees and plants. Horsedrawn carriages are a good way of touring all the local sights like the Pasaje de las Chinitas, the home of local flamenco, and the bullring which is open to visitors when nothing is going on.

There are plenty of hotels in addition to the *parador* with its views across the city, the nearby docks and the Mediterranean. Some of the best fish restaurants are in the Paseo Maritimo, with a large covered

*Torremolinos has plenty of souvenirs and refreshments for sale along the front*

market not far from the river. However there is no doubt that the city's neighbours along the coast have more to offer holidaymakers who only want to relax in the sun and enjoy themselves.

It has become increasingly fashionable to sneer at the Costa del Sol. This is a pity because visitors can opt for exactly the kind of holiday that appeals to them, whether it entails exploring the inland areas where tourists are few and far between, spending all day beside a swimming pool at a private villa or joining the crowds along the seafront. Menus in two or three different languages are invaluable for people who have to be careful about what they eat and drink and it is reassuring to know that if one needs a doctor, dentist or oculist he is quite likely to speak English. The same applies to chemists who can usually deal with minor ailments on the spot. Some newsagents sell London morning newspapers towards evening on the same day, Gibraltar Radio links up with the BBC's General Overseas Service at regular intervals and it is possible to watch a number of popular British programmes on television. Finally, in the unlikely event of any serious trouble some two dozen different countries, including Britain and Canada, have consular representatives in Málaga.

The first and oldest of the coastal resorts to the west of the capital is **Torremolinos**, once the city's fishing quarter but now an independent municipality consisting of interminable highrise blocks, streets inundated with advertisements and shops bursting at the seams with every type of merchandise. It is difficult to believe that there were hardly any buildings in Torremolinos 25 to 30 years ago, apart from the old water mills that gave the town its name and a collection of fishermen's cottages in La Carihuela. However it is still possible to discover a few relics from the past tucked away among the concrete and plate glass.

One example of this is the old baker's shop in the Plaza Costa del Sol which opened its doors in 1880 and continued to bake its own bread on the premises until 1964. The Torre de Pimentel, on the Calle San Miguel, dates back to the fourteenth century and was probably built by the Arabs. At all events it was known as the Torre de los Molinos on account of the water mills which only stopped functioning in 1924. One or two quite large, but much younger, houses have survived, including the Villa Pepita on the Avenida del Lido, built in 1925 with Moorish overtones that would probably look more at home in the Plaza de España in Sevilla. Another worth mentioning is the Hacienda San Miguel in the Calle Doña María Barbino, with beautiful Venetian ceilings and an Italian marble staircase. It was once surrounded by large gardens but lost the greater part of its grounds to farsighted developers in 1940.

The centre of the old town was the Calle San Miguel, now almost lost in a welter of boutiques and restaurants, flamenco bars, discos, shops and small workshops turning out a variety of crafts and souvenirs. There are facilities for all the usual aquatic sports, with small boats and other equipment for hire, in addition to riding and hunting further inland, tennis and golf. Other attractions include bullfights and a wax museum. The hotels are many and various, from large and excellently appointed to modest and retiring, but even some of the less obtrusive ones have their own tennis courts and swimming pools.

It is extremely difficult to tell where Torremolinos ends and **Benalmádena Costa** begins. It has the same type of beaches, plenty of hotels and apartment blocks and is inundated with restaurants, cafés and every type of shop. In addition to all this there is a casino and a golf course at Torrequebrada and the ruins of a Moorish watch tower guarding the entrance to an extensive marina which was started in 1972. It is now more like a suburb in its own right with moorings for up to one thousand boats and every facility for yachtsmen, along with apartment blocks, restaurants, wide streets and ample parking space for cars. Quite close by is the Castillo Bil-Bil on the Carretera de Cádiz, dating from 1932, but now converted into a combined culture centre and exhibition hall. It also includes the tourist office.

Half a mile up the hillside an area known as **Arroyo la Miel** was originally the home of farmers and fishermen but now has its full quota of highrise buildings, shops, supermarkets and private villas as well as a railway station on the line from Málaga to Fuengirola. Its chief holiday attraction is the Tivoli World Amusement Park with everything that its name implies.

Further up the road is **Benalmádena Pueblo**, the little mountain village which gave birth to the whole holiday complex. It was probably Phoenician in origin and was certainly occupied by the Romans, but owes its name to the Arabs who called it simply Sons of the Mines. The village has its own bullring where events are staged throughout the winter and a small archaeological museum full of exhibits discovered in the vicinity. Time has not really changed the narrow, winding streets lined with demure white houses to any great extent, except when coachloads of sightseers make their way through the Plaza de España to the old church perched on a rocky outcrop to the south. It has its own little restaurants, a variety of small shops including a supermarket, an open air market every Friday and a good road through the mountains to Mijas less than 10km (6 miles) away.

The town of **Mijas**, cradled in the hills above Fuengirola, insists that it was once part of the fabled kingdom of *Tartessus* and that a section of the early fortifications can still be seen in one of the old walls. That is as it may be, but the original settlement does appear to have been ignored by the passing Phoenicians, Romans and Visigoths although it was overrun by the Saracens and occupied by Omar Ben Afsun before the Christians regained control of Andalucía. Unfortunately the official archives were mislaid a long time ago so local historians have had to rely on stories handed down from one generation to the next. This does not make for a high degree of accuracy but at least it helps to keep the best legends alive.

As recently as 1961 the only way up to Mijas was along a donkey trail through the mountains from Benalmádena. By the 1970s there

*The donkey taxi service at Mijas is a popular tourist attraction*

*A Mijas craftsman making marquetry wares outside his shop*

*A garlic seller pedalling his wares in Mijas*

*Mimosa adds a splash of colour in the spring*

was a road linking the hill village with its coastal suburbs, the first visitors were booking in to its new hotel and Lew Hoad's tennis club was in operation. Today it is one of the largest municipalities on the Costa del Sol with foreign residents outnumbering the indigenous population, while information from the local council is available in more than eight different languages. Classes are held in everything from Spanish for beginners to computer programming and, apart from all the usual sports facilities visitors can learn to sail at the Nautic Club of Mijas Costa, hang glide, practice judo or play hockey on roller skates.

The Church of the Immaculate Conception was built in the early seventeenth century on the site of an ancient castle, incorporating one of the original towers as a belfry. It shares the old walled section, once known as the Plaza de la Villa, but later renamed La Muralla, with a modern auditorium and the local bullring which is nearly 100 years old. The practice of bullrunning through the streets was revived in 1979 and is now an annual event which takes place at dawn on 8 September during the festival in honour of Our Lady of the Rock.

According to legend the Virgen de la Peña was discovered in 1586 in the ruins of an old castle, which was converted shortly afterwards into a Carmelite monastery. Both have now disappeared apart from a vestige of the old walls and a cave which is the Virgin's current sanctuary, lit by candles and festooned with votive offerings. On one side the balustrade commands a magnificent view across to the Mediterranean while on the other a depression, until recently filled with olive trees, was transformed into the Plaza Virgen de la Peña in 1983. It is surrounded by restaurants and good many little shops selling everything from typically down-market souvenirs to leather goods and wooden articles such as musical boxes, chess boards and trays inlaid with contrasting materials. Handmade carpets are another cottage industry that has grown and prospered, receiving orders from all over the world.

At one end of the Plaza Virgen de la Peña the famous donkey taxis, introduced as a tourist gimmick in the 1960s, wait to take visitors for trips round the old town. Anyone who does not feel up to actually riding a donkey can choose between little box-like carts, just about big enough for two people, or slightly larger open carriages drawn by horses or mules. More energetic sightseers can visit any of the outlying hermitages such as San Antón, built by a group of sailors who were saved from drowning in the eighteenth century, where there is a service for the blessing of animals in mid-January and a well attended pilgrimage in May.

A good fast road connects Mijas with its suburbs at sea level and together they have a large selection of hotels and hostels, furnished villas and apartments and three different campsites. Apart from Lew Hoad's Rancho de Tenis and an 18-hole golf course there is the Parque Acuatico Mijas, a large amusement centre surrounded by gardens with more than twenty different types of water slides, pools and sandy patches that provides entertainment for everyone. It also has a self-service restaurant, a bar and a gift shop selling some quite useful items as well as the inevitable souvenirs.

**Fuengirola**, which blends in very happily with Mijas Costa, is almost a carbon copy of the other large seaside resorts. However it is a good deal older, having been founded by the Romans when it was known as *Suel*. The town lies at the entrance to a shallow valley surrounded by hills and has a promenade following the curving beaches for a distance of 7km (4 miles), which makes it the longest on the coast. The first of these is Carvajal, a spot favoured rather more by Spanish residents than foreign visitors. Beyond it the fishing village of Los Boliches was once separated from Fuengirola by a small river but this has run dry, except after exceptionally heavy storms, so the district is now considered to be part of the main town. The name was derived from the Bolicheros, merchant sailors from Genoa who settled there in the early fourteenth century. They are remembered especially every July during the Fiesta de la Virgen del Carmen, who is the patron saint of fishermen. There are still a few old buildings on the Paseo Maritimo, one or two typical Spanish bars tucked away out of sight and a group of Roman columns in the Plaza Castilla.

Fuengirola has its full compliment of hotels and apartment blocks, shops, cafés and restaurants as well as one or two delightful little squares. The Museo Abierto de Pintura is a unique art gallery because, instead of being housed in an ancient mansion, it consists of enormous coloured murals painted high up on the outside walls of several different buildings in the centre of the town. The zoo, the only one currently on the Costa del Sol, has well over 300 animals in addition to a children's playground.

The Salon Varietes claims to be the only theatre in Spain providing continuous entertainments for the English speaking community. It opened in 1985 and has never looked back. The season lasts from mid-September to mid-June. Tuesday's large open-air market is the place to look for bargains where stallholders expect to argue about the price and may well knock 20 per cent or more off expensive articles.

One of the most oustanding landmarks overlooking the highway

*A horse and carriage patiently waits for custom at Fuengirola*

*The harbour, Fuengirola*

*Fuengirola's fishermen putting the world to right*

*The open-air market at Fuengirola is the largest on the Costa del Sol*

to Marbella is **Sohail Castle**, the remains of a Moorish stronghold  built by Abd-ar-Rahman III, caliph of Córdoba, in the tenth century. It was captured by the Catholic Monarchs in 1487 and restored by Charles V to serve as one of his main defences on the coast. Napoleon had the same idea during the Peninsular War and one or two of the small cannon he was forced to leave behind can still be seen on the promenade.

**Marbella**, some 27km (17 miles) from Fuengirola, is generally regarded as the most up market of all the coastal resorts along the Costa del Sol. It was lived in by the Iberians, visited by the Phoenicians, the Greeks, the Vandals and the Visigoths besides being a stopping place for Romans on the Via Augusta and a well-fortified Arab town. A variety of prehistoric relics have been found in the cave of Pecho Redondo. The Romans contributed a bridge over the Nagueles stream while a section of the protective walls and towers built by the Moors can still be seen in the old quarter of the town. The ancient Alcázar, dating from the ninth century and incorporating a few Roman remains, was rebuilt at the time of Ferdinand and Isabel but later it fell on hard times and is now in grave danger of disintegrating altogether. However plans are afoot to restore the whole fortress, even removing a few of the surrounding houses to give it room to breathe and make it easier to floodlight in the evenings.

Chief among the buildings added after the Reconquest are the Hospital of San Juan de Dios, two elderly sanctuaries, the Bazán Hospital and a brace of sixteenth-century convents. Considerably younger, but interesting for quite different reasons, is the modern casino in the Andalucía Plaza Hotel. The area has something of interest for everyone, apart from hotels, restaurants and a delightful seafront, such as hunting reserves up in the mountains, outstanding golf courses, well-equipped marinas, bullrings, fishing boats for hire and quite a few individual beaches. There are also buses up to **Ojén**, known principally for its panoramic views, a local liqueur spiced with fennel, an up-market hunting lodge and the traditional festivals held during the second week in October.

**San Pedro de Alcántara**, slightly further down the coast but still part of the municipality of Marbella, has its own memories from the past. The remains of the Roman colony of *Silniana* include a collection of mosaics and the thermal baths of Las Bóvedas while the basilica of Vega del Mar in Linda Vista was used as a necropolis by the Visigoths. Today, the main attraction is liable to be the **Puerto Banús** marina, full of expensive pleasure craft with some attractive private apartments and delightful small restaurants.

Marinas, golf courses and hunting reserves are constantly recurring features along this part of the Costa del Sol. **Estepona**, which has not yet borne the full brunt of development, has a large harbour with one of the biggest fishing fleets on the coast, moorings for 900 pleasure craft, a unique bullring and three 18-hole golf courses.

The Moorish town of *Estebbuna* replaced an earlier Roman settlement of which very little remains apart from the Aqueduct of Salduba, now open only to people engaged in serious research. This whole region is ideal walking country, full of fauna and flora. There are no marked footpaths at the moment but the national conservation authorities are planning a series of trails through the nature reserve for people who enjoy exploring in this type of country.

Estepona dates very largely from the nineteenth century and takes its pleasures rather more quietly than the brasher resorts. Early risers can watch the catch being auctioned at the fish exchange dock in the harbour, conditions are excellent for sailing, windsurfing and underwater fishing and the beaches of La Rada and El Cristo, although busy during the season, are not usually overcrowded. The Costa Natura was the first nudist beach to be officially recognised by the authorities but it is not quite so unique these days when topless sunbathing takes place almost everywhere. The main celebration is the Festival of the Virgen del Carmen, the patron saint of fishermen, on 16 July.

The last place of interest before the border with Cádiz is **Manilva** which is not really a coastal resort at all, although it does have a beach near the castle of San Luis de Sabinillas, also known as the Palace of the Duchess. The village itself has a river frontage, the remnants of a Roman spa, some natural sulphur springs and particularly good grapes which account for the annual wine festival in early September.

From Manilva the road continues to follow the river up to **Casares** which, in spite of all the formidable competition, describes itself as the most photogenic village in Spain. It is one of the famous 'white towns' with a ruined fortress up on the hill and traces of an even older Iberian settlement at Alesipe quite close by. The houses, some with wrought iron grilles over the windows, clamber over each other up the hillside along narrow streets that bear witness to their Arab origins, calling at the Church of San Sebastián, built in the seventeenth century. It is essentially a farming community with olive groves, vineyards and vegetable gardens as well as attractive views down to the coast some 16km (10 miles) away. There is an alternative route back to the sea which joins the main highway below Estepona while the first road presses on northwards to Gaucín.

Like all its contemporaries **Gaucín** has had a somewhat chequered existance. After being a Roman frontier post it fell into Moorish hands and acquired its Castillo del Aguila, or Eagle's Castle, in the thirteenth century before being recaptured by the Christians nearly

*Marbella's new exclusive apartment blocks are distinctly modernistic*

*Puerto Banús, west of Marbella is now the fashionable centre of the Costa del Sol*

*The beach at Marbella*

←

200 years later. But that was by no means the extent of its problems. During a furious battle in 1309 Guzmán the Good, who talked his way into history at the siege of Tarifa, was killed in an attempt to capture the fortress. Unfortunately it was accidentally blown up in 1848 and never repaired. During the nineteenth century the town was popular with both outlaws and travellers bound for Gibraltar, the latter spending the night at the local inn which still allows visitors to inspect its old hotel register. Still more recently the village played a small, but not particularly enviable role, during the Spanish Civil War.

**Algatocín**, 6km (4 miles) away on the road to Ronda, has nothing much to offer apart from a sixteenth-century church that was rebuilt 200 years ago and a scenic route through the Cortes de la Frontera nature reserve to Ubrique in Cádiz province. There are also some alternative small roads through grasslands, where the verges occasionally break out in a rash of wild flowers like sweet peas and dog roses, to such isolated hill towns as Jubrique, set in woodlands with two old hermitages and a nearby campsite on the banks of the Río Genal.

The rather larger road carries on regardless to **Benadalid** which is equally self-effacing, although the small cemetery is worth a casual glance on account of all the funeral niches lining the remaining walls of a fortress built during the Moorish occupation. After this the route lies mainly through olive trees and vineyards, with an occasional glimpse of an ancient tower presiding over its own whitewashed houses, until it reaches Ronda, the last and one of the most spectacular of all the 'white towns'.

Although there are several different ways of getting to Ronda most people drive up through the mountains from San Pedro de Alcántara on the coast less than 50km (31 miles) away. After a rather bumpy start it becomes an exceptionally good road, taking all the valleys and ravines in its stride with a number of places where motorists can pull off to admire the view. On a clear day this may well include Gibraltar and the coast of North Africa but it can also be spectacular when the sea mist starts rolling in, leaving the mountain peaks floating on a silver-grey cloud. At first sight **Ronda** is a trifle disappointing, a collection of almost-white buildings in the middle of a small plateau with little apparently to justify its reputation.

In the early days the town was an Iberian settlement known as *Arunda*, which the Romans changed to *Munda*. With the arrival of the Moors the town emerged as the centre of an Arab kingdom, so well fortified that it took a large Christian force and a cunning ruse by Ferdinand to capture it in 1485. During the centuries that followed

Ronda suffered just as many changes of fortune as any other mountain stronghold, culminating in the Civil War. There seems to have been little to choose between the atrocities perpetrated by the Republicans and those committed by the Nationalists if one listens to the reminiscences of some of the older inhabitants, who are still decidedly partisan in their views.

The first signs of antiquity to be seen on the approach road up to the ramparts are the fifteenth-century church of Espíritu Santo and the Convent of San Francisco built shortly afterwards. Beyond the Arab Puerta del Almocábar, consisting of a horseshoe arch flanked by matching towers, and its companion Gate of Carlos V, the old quarter is full of small, interlocking streets with the Plaza de la Duquesa de Parcent up on the left-hand side. Here the town council has taken over the seventeenth-century barracks, facing the Convent of Santa Clara and looking obliquely across the central gardens to the Collegiate Church of Santa María la Mayor. This was built on the site of an ancient mosque of which nothing remains apart from a closed archway just beyond the entrance. Inside there are two Baroque altars, one drenched in gold and the other beautifully carved in wood surrounded by tiled surfaces that look as though they might have been borrowed from a gigantic chessboard. There is also some fine carving in the stalls, an ancient Bible and a few not very outstanding paintings and murals. The sacristan lives next door behind an arcade and overlooked by a tower that replaced the original minaret.

A short walk away the Casa Mondragón was an Arab palace adapted for use by Ferdinand and Isabel before being altered and restored at frequent intervals and eventually earmarked as the home for exhibitions and a new archaeological museum. Both it and the small square nearby have splendid views from the top of the ravine down into the valley below. Foremost among its more elderly neighbours is the so-called House of the Giants which is, in fact, a Moorish acropolis with decorations added at the same time as those of the Alhambra. At the opposite end of this rocky spur, on the far side of the main through-road, there is a free standing minaret left over from a mosque and beyond it the 400-year-old Salvatierre Palace that was fully restored in the eighteenth century. It is still a private residence, but occasionally allows visitors inside provided they make an appointment beforehand. A stone's throw away more than 300 steps, called the Mina, were carved out of the rock face down to the old Arab bridge over the Río Guadalevin and the carefully restored Arab baths. Other places in the vicinity are the Palace of the Moorish king which, despite its name and a portrait in tiles on the outer wall, was only built in the early seventeenth century, and the

*Estepona still maintains a large fishing fleet and net mending is a necessary task*

*Punta de la Chullera, west of Estepona, where the coast becomes less developed*

*The yacht marina at Estepona*

←

neighbouring Convent of Santo Domingo, once occupied by the Inquisition.

A narrow gorge, up to 100m (330ft) deep in some places, and called El Tajo, separates the ancient town from its marginally younger relation on the other side. The Arabs took the line of least resistance and built their bridge at the bottom. The Puento Viejo appeared in the seventeenth century and was followed, after one disasterous attempt that collapsed in less than a decade, by the present New Bridge, crossing the top of the ravine and completed in 1793. It is a magnificent structure with a bloodthirsty history.

The road over the New Bridge leads directly to the Plaza de España and on to the Plaza de Toros with its superb stone bullring, founded in the reign of Philip II, rebuilt in the eighteenth century, and said to be the largest in Spain. It was intended originally as a place where the local nobility could perfect the art of bullfighting on horseback but when this was frowned on by the Bourbon kings some other system had to be devised to take its place. Francisco Romero, who was born in Ronda in 1698, worked out a complicated set of rules for the matador, who would in future fight on foot, and invented the red *muleta* and the short sword that are used in the closing stages. His son, Juan, added a number of dramatic touches such as the *cuadrilla* (the colourful team of assistants) leaving his grandson Pedro, who is still considered to be one of the greatest of all Spanish bullfighters, to put them into practice.

A small but extremely fascinating museum, tucked away under the tiers of seats, includes posters announcing the fights scheduled for May 1785, pictures of some very early events, magnificent capes and richly embroidered suits of lights worn by the matadors. Each September this cradle of bullfighting stages a special Corrido Goyesca in honour of Pedro Romero with every detail, including the costumes, designed to create a faithful reproduction of the scheme that would have been familiar to the painter Francisco de Goya some 200 years ago.

There is a small park quite close to the bullring with an impressive view over the valley, in addition to a whole variety of little shops, cafés and restaurants serving traditional dishes and snacks. Foremost among the hotels is the Reina Victoria which played host to the German poet Rainer Maria Rilke and has kept his room unchanged as a very modest museum.

It is well worth exploring both sections of the town on foot, discovering a number of other small churches, the monument to Pedro Romero, the narrow streets lined with typical old houses and even a large trough still used on occasions for doing the family laundry. However it is rather a demanding walk along the Camino de los Molinos below the rock face, even taking a shortcut down from the Plaza Campillo, in order to get the best overall view of the New Bridge which has become the trade mark of the town.

There are several places of interest within easy reach of Ronda such as the Dolmen of Chopo near the turning off to Grazalema in Cádiz province, the Cave of El Gato not far from the centre of Benaoján and the Cueve de la Pileta further down the same road. This contains a number of simple cave drawings thought to be about 25,000 years old. Among the discoveries made in the caves were weapons and bones from the Bronze Age and pieces of Neolithic pottery, claimed, as usual, to be the oldest of their kind yet found in Europe. By comparison the Roman town of *Acinipo* is a positive newcomer. The ruins, known as Ronda la Vieja, are about 12km (7 miles) west of the city and consist mainly of granite walls surrounding the remains of a fairly large theatre.

There are several roads leading away from Ronda. One goes to San Roque and Gibraltar, another heads for Jerez de la Frontera and Cádiz while two more make contact with the main highway through Antequera to Granada. A fifth wanders off in the direction of El Burgo on its way to Málaga, stopping at **Coín**, a busy market town in the valley of the Guadalhorce. This is another centre with distinctive Moorish overtones in the form of a fifteenth-century Alcázar and  picturesque old quarters, mainly in the vicinity of the Plaza de San Andrés with its sixteenth-century church. Most activity is concentrated round the large covered market, designed mainly as a wholesale centre for fruit and vegetables. There are one or two fairly basic inns with the added attraction of organised donkey safaris up into the Sierra Albuquería. Coín celebrates often and enthusiastically starting with processions during Holy Week. A large percentage of the town is decked out in style for the Crosses of May competitions after which people from all over the area join in a pilgrimage in honour of their patron saint at the end of the month. August is the time of the Flamenco Festival while folklore comes into its own when song and dance contests are held in December.

**Tolox**, a small Arab-style town in the foothills of the Serranía de Ronda has won a number of official beauty prizes but is known mainly for the spa of Fuente Amargura. The mineral waters of this natural spring are said to be particularly helpful for anyone who has trouble with their breathing. The village has its own little byway leading off the main road, some rather basic inns and hillsides covered with Spanish firs.

Almost the same distance from Coín in the opposite direction,

←*The 'white town' of Casares*

*Casares claims to be the most photogenic village in Spain*

*Gateway leading to the Roman Bridge at Ronda*

**Alhaurín el Grande** is old and somewhat larger than one would expect. The Iberians left nothing of interest behind them but it does have some modest Roman remains. The Arabs contributed a few towers and an archway called El Cobertizo, but their mosque was replaced by the Church of the Incarnation in the sixteenth century.

There is a good deal to see between Alhaurin el Grande and Málaga city a little over 30km (19 miles) away. **Alhaurín de la Torre**, known to the Romans as *Lauro Vetus*, was where Julius Caesar's legions put an end to Pompey's ambitions by cutting off his head. Today the village, like all its companions in the Valley of Orange Blossom, is much more interested in its citrus farms, avocados and the Torre del Canta celebrations which it describes as the most important flamenco festival in the world.

**Churriana**, somewhat closer to the capital and to the Málaga-Cádiz highway, owes its existence to the Phoenicians who established a trading post near La Loma de San Julián in about the seventh century BC. The oldest of its more recent attractions is El Retiro, an estate that belonged to the Bishop of Málaga in the seventeenth century. A hundred years later the new owner, the Count of Villalcázar, laid out a series of landscaped gardens with ornamental stairways, balustrades, marble statues, waterfalls and fountains. More than 600 trees and flowering shrubs were planted and these have survived rather better than the stonework which has suffered badly from neglect and a lack of water. Plans are now under way to restore the whole property as a world centre for the protection of plants, birds and animals. Eventually the palace will be used as a research centre with a restaurant open to visitors, a children's playground and other services.

Younger by about 200 years is Los Jardines de la Cónsula, built in 1856 by the Prussian consul in Málaga but far better known as the house where Ernest Hemingway did much of his writing. The mansion now belongs to the Málaga City Council who used it originally for official receptions. With extensive building work under way it has ceased to be a tourist attraction. Finally there is La Concepción, famous for its collection of tropical and sub tropical plants and flowers and reputed to be one of the largest of its kind in Europe. Churriana has a comfortable hotel, some small inns and furnished accommodation of various descriptions as well as regular bus services to both Málaga and Torremolinos.

North of Alhaurín el Grande a good road pushes its way through citrus farms to Cartama, where there are some not very outstanding Moorish ruins, and on to Pizarra. From here the main route continues to Antequera but an excellent alternative, given the necessary time, branches off to **Alora**. This is another typical Andalucían village with Roman connections, a sixteenth-century fortress, the remains of its medieval walls and narrow, beautifully preserved alleys climbing up the hillside between rows of rather bland white houses.

The impressive El Chorro Gorge, a canyon some 400m (1,300ft) deep in places, lies between Alora and Ardales, eaten away by the Río Guadalhorce as it froths and foams its way through the ravine. The railway negotiates Los Gaitanes Pass, twisting in and out of a series of tunnels and giving its passengers some brief, though spectacular, views. However there is a great deal more to explore by car. At the El Chorro railway siding, consisting of a few houses, a small tavern and a large reservoir, it is possible to see El Camino del Rey, the famous King's Path, stapled to the side of a naked cliff. Rather easier to pick out is a narrow concrete water shute leading down from a tower-like structure on the hilltop high above. The path was built at the same time as the hydro-electric system and was in a fit state to receive a royal visit when the project was officially opened in 1921. However it has now been allowed to deteriorate very badly and is extremely dangerous. The bridge over the gorge is in a shocking state, but as some people insist on inspecting it at close quarters the authorities are discussing what to do about it when they finalise their plans for a large campsite in the Ardales nature reserve. The three man-made lakes above the gorge with their extensive beaches backed by pine forests are already popular with both fishermen and holidaymakers and the idea is to add a new campsite with a control office, a car park, a youth hostel and even a heliport.

Beyond El Chorro a well signposted road climbs up to Bobastro, known as The Impregnable a thousand years ago when it is thought to have been the capital of a rebel kingdom established by Omar Ben Hafsun in opposition to the caliph of Córdoba. The city, if it ever really existed, has now completely disappeared apart from a few odd ruins and a unique ninth-century church carved out of solid rock where legend insists that Hafsun is buried. There is another large reservoir on the top of the mountain with spectacular views down on to the tower above El Chorro that suddenly looks small enough to fit into a matchbox.

The whole area appears to have been well populated in prehistoric times but the Cave of Doña Trinidad Grund, roughly 4km (2 miles) from Ardales, only came to light in 1821 after an earthquake. There are several large underground caverns resplendent with stalactites and stalagmites while one in particular, called El Calvario, has some very interesting Paleolithic wall paintings. The caves were named after a well known socialite who lived in **Carratraca**, a small but very

*Ronda: the Church of Santa María la Mayor*

*←The New Bridge completed in 1793 spans the El Tajo gorge at Ronda*

popular local spa. Its waters were thought to be so beneficial that King Ferdinand VII had a special retreat built for himself and his family, but no-one seems to know if he ever made use of it. This has been turned into a pleasant hostel for people who want to soak themselves in the hot mineral waters for the sake of their health. The house that once belonged to Doña Trinidad Grund has been transformed into the town hall, but apart from this the only tourist attraction is the oddly shaped bullring set back against the rocky slope of the Sierra Blanquilla.

Ardales itself is said to have been a Stone Age settlement before the Iberians moved in and called it *Turobriga*. The Romans built a small fortress on the site but there is practically nothing to see apart from a few rather uninteresting ruins. With very little else to inspect in the vicinity the best plan is to take the road from Carratraca to Alora and then head north to Antequera.

The town of **Antequera**, some 50km (31 miles) due north of Málaga city, is a most delightful place, standing on the edge of a fertile plain with enough tourist attractions to make it worthwhile spending a day or two here. It started life as a prehistoric settlement before the Romans took an interest in it and founded a town called *Antikaria*. They were followed by the Moors and later by the Christians, all of whom left ample proof of their existence.

The oldest structure is the prehistoric Cueva de Menga dating from about 2500BC. It consists of a large oval chamber of twenty-five vertical stones with three rough oblong columns helping to support the massive stone slabs that form the roof. Each one of them weighs several tons, while the largest stone block is said to tip the scales at 180 tons. It is thought to have been a type of warriors' burial chamber but sadly it was looted a very long time ago. The Cueva del Viera, younger by about 100 years, is very similar, although it is smaller and more finely finished with a small tomb at the far end, whereas the Cueva del Romeral has been described as the first example of true architecture in Spain with a false dome constructed in 2000BC.

Until quite recently it was thought that no important Roman ruins had survived, but in 1988 the remains of some ancient baths were uncovered next door to the Church of Santa María la Mayor. It was considerably likely that the large pool which had suddenly come to light was part of the public baths of *Antikaria*. Meanwhile an exceptionally well preserved Roman villa, discovered on a site at Grallumbar, is thought to have been involved in the production of olive oil, but so far it is not open to visitors.

The Moors, who changed the name of the town to *Antakira*, built their *alcazabar*, with its Tower of Allegiance, at the top of the hill but, although well fortified, it was captured in 1410 by a royal princeling who was known thereafter as Fernando del Antequera. The Christians did not start building very seriously until the early sixteenth century when they put up the Collegiate Church of San Sebastián and the Church of Santa María la Mayor with a monumental façade inspired by a Roman triumphal arch. The Church of Carmen is worth seeing for its Mudéjar ceiling and three massive altarpieces, but for sheer curiosity none of them can rival the Church of Los Remedios whose Virgin is patron saint of the town.

Quite apart from several other churches Antequera has a number of elderly mansions, one of which is home to the Municipal Museum.  With its grand staircase and cloistered courtyard the Nájera Palace makes an ideal setting for a number of very worthwhile exhibits including several paintings, a carving of St Francis of Assisi by Pedro de Mena and a Roman statue of a young boy, cast in bronze in the first century AD and known as the Efebo de Antequera. Further excavations are still going on to the west of the town where it is thought that there was an even larger Roman settlement, judging from the amphitheatre with seating for some 8,000 people.

With so much evidence of an illustrious past Antequera could be forgiven for resting on its laurels but nothing could be further from the truth. It has a go-ahead shopping centre, cars have outstripped the available parking spaces, old crafts are being revived and agriculture has been intensified with the introduction of modern farming methods. Its celebrations start with religious processions during Holy Week, followed by a Spring Fair at the end of May, a Royal Fair during the third week of August and the Feast Day of Nuestra Señora de los Remedios on 8 September.

Peculiar rock formations are by no means uncommon in the  Antequera region. The town itself is overlooked by an oddly-shaped mountain known as the Peña de los Enamorados, or Lovers' Rock, because a young couple, separated by religion, are said to have hurled themselves from one of the peaks about 1,000 years ago. Even more strange are the weird images, sculptured by time and the weather, in the El Torcal nature reserve about 15km (9 miles) further south. To some people the towering limestone outcrops look like a fantastic cartoon city with crooked towers and tortured alleyways; to others they appear to be unearthly figures and incredible animals from the realms of mythology. It is a lonely, deserted area where vultures circle overhead, lizards bask in the sun, ready to beat a hasty retreat into the nearest deep stone crevice, and the wind moans softly through the tangle of narrow passages. Because it would be very easy to get lost a number of trails have been marked with arrows and

*A wayside shrine near Coín*

*The small town of Coín is a centre for selling the fruit and vegetables grown in the surrounding countryside*

*Monda, a quiet town in the hills above the Costa del Sol*

→

there is a hunters' lodge which will provide additional information.

Before turning south again it would be a pity not to visit **Archidona**, slightly off the main route to Granada. It is a good deal smaller than Antequera but its history is no less impressive, going back to the time when the Phoenicians referred to it as *Oscua*. The Romans took it over and renamed it *Arx Domina*, but it was left to the Arabs to provide the town with its own Emir in the person of Ad-Al-Rhaman in 756. Apart from the Plaza Ochavada, a beautiful octagonal square built 200 years ago, there are the remains of an ancient castle and part of the medieval walls as well as the churches of Las Monjas Mínimas and Santa Ana. The Virgen de Gracia lives in a hermitage on the site of the old town in what was once an Arab mosque. Enough columns are still standing to justify its claim to be the only one of its kind left in Málaga and, with perhaps less accuracy, that it may be the oldest on view anywhere in Europe. As the Virgen de Gracia is the patron saint of Archidona the town's main celebration always begins with a pilgrimage to her shrine at midnight on 14 August, leaving everyone time to get back for the festivities the following morning.

The interior of Axarquia, a wedge-shaped region to the east of Málaga city, bounded largely by the Mediterranean and the mountainous fringe of Granada, seldom sees visitors let alone tourists. Not so long ago it was bandit country but now there are many excellent reasons for taking to the hills, away from the hustle and bustle of the coastal belt. In the meantime, the main route out of Málaga follows the shoreline to **Rincón de la Victoria**, originally a small fishing village that is building furiously in an effort to catch up with Torremolinos and Benalmádena. At first glance there is not a great deal to recommend it but on closer inspection it turns out to have long brownish beaches, the ruined castle of Bezmiliana and delicious small clams called *coquina*. According to Pliny this was the site of the Temple of the Moon, long gone but not forgotton. On the other hand the Cueva del Tesoro, some 2km (1 mile) from the town, is where the five Mohammedian kings are said to have hidden their treasures. In recent times the resort has added a comfortable hotel, a few inns, furnished apartments, an 18-hole golf course, riding stables, tennis courts and fishing boats for hire.

A few kilometres further along the coast a small, twisted byway, struggles up to **Macharaviaya** before petering out altogether. The hamlet, surrounded by olive and almond trees, is all that remains of a town that was known some 200 years ago as Little Madrid. In those days it was a thriving community, due largely to the Gálves family who are just as well known in America as they are in Spain. José de

Gálvez was an orphan who worked his way up to become a favourite at the court of Charles III. The king was so impressed by his ability that he dubbed José as Marqués de Sonora and promoted him to the post of Minister of the Indies. In this capacity he controlled the Spanish possessions in the New World with ruthless efficiency, extending his sphere of influence well into California and other southern regions of the USA. His brother Matías became the Viceroy of New Spain while his nephew Bernardo took care of the military side, fighting with equal enthusiasm against the Apache Indians and later the British forces during the American War of Independence. Galveston in Texas, took its name from the family while Macharaviaya, not to be outdone, returned the compliment by putting up new street signs like Pensacola.

The large and now extremely world-weary church was built by José de Gálvez in 1785 and filled with appropriate treasures to the delight of the townspeople who earned a very respectable living in a local factory when it was given the sole right to market its stamps on the other side of the Atlantic. But the good times ended as suddenly as they began and all that now remains are the marble tombs and alabaster statues in the crypt. Titles like the Viscount of Galveston died out with the last of the line whose founder eventually returned home to be buried in his grey marble mausoleum.

After negotiating the same little road back to the coast the next place of interest is **Torre del Mar** which is convinced that it was once part of *Mainake*, a Greek settlement that was destroyed by the Carthaginians long before the Romans arrived. With nothing tangible to back up its claims the resort is more interested in the future than it is in the past. All its efforts are concentrated on building highrise apartment blocks and maintaining one of the widest and longest promenades on the Costa del Sol. This extends as far as Caleta de Vélez, the only fishing port with a marina on Málaga's eastern seaboard. The area is ideal for all types of water sports, small pleasure craft are available for hire and fishermen are in their element. The resort is also famous for its seafood, particularly varieties grilled with lemon.

Torre del Mar is also the holiday playground for **Vélez-Málaga**, the capital of the region situated up in the hills a few kilometres away. Although the town is quite sure that it was built over the remains of *Mainake* its name is derived from *Ballix-Malace* (rock fortress), and as such it was highly regarded by the Moors before the Catholic Monarchs snatched it back in 1487. Today it is a pleasant market town in the fertile Vélez Valley with the Torre del Homenaje and a few walls that were once part of the Alcázar. The Church of

*The Plaza Ochavada, Archidona*

*Primitive agricultural methods can sometimes still be seen in Andalucía*

Santa María la Mayor was the first building to be put up by the victorious Christians who imported its main altarpiece from Rome in the early sixteenth century. There are a few other elderly churches and palaces, including one which belonged to the Marqués de Veniel which is now the town hall, and some atmospheric old quarters such as the Arrabal de San Sebastián and the Barrio de la Villa.

For those who prefer to avoid the coast road there are other ways of reaching the heart of Axarquia, one of them being the ancient highway to Granada. There is a lot of magnificent scenery and several interesting old places to visit but it is just as well to have a good map and be prepared for some very questionable minor roads through the mountains. For example, a backway out of Colmenar, in the direction of the Puerto de los Alazores, leads past an isolated white building called the Antigua Venta de Alfarnate. This claims to be the oldest tavern in Andalucía where both travellers and bandits used to stop for refreshments at the end of the seventeenth century.

From the far side of the Puerto de los Alazores a lonely byway makes for Zafarraya and joins a larger road at the Ventas de Zafarraya, the site of another well known inn. Travelling south, the route bypasses Alcaucín, where some of Napoleon's troops were stationed during the Peninsular War, and continues in a rather more sedate fashion to Vélez-Málaga.

Back on the coast the next place of interest is **Algarrobo**, slightly inland from the fishing port of La Caleta de Vélez. It is a typical whitewashed Andalucían hamlet with an eighteenth-century church, the hermitage of San Sebastián, a few exceedingly sparse remnants of a tenth-century village and just a trace of some prehistoric tombs at Morro de Trayamar. Another small scenic road winds its way up to Cómpeta, poised on its own hillside with a thriving pottery and some prolific vineyards that provide the ingredients for its annual Night of Wine. With nowhere else to go the road doubles back to the quiet, self-effacing town of Torrox before rejoining the coastal highway shortly before a well signposted turning off to Frigiliana.

**Frigiliana**, the last white hill village before the border with Granada, is a charming little place where donkeys plod patiently along the narrow streets, the balconies are filled with flowers and the gobble of turkeys blends well with the sound of flamenco music. Parts of the town, snuggled up against the hillside, have hardly changed since Moorish times, but the twentieth century makes its presence felt in the form of restaurants, craft shops and a treacle factory which the residents insist is the only one in Spain. The surrounding countryside was the scene of one of the last major battles between Christians and Moors, an event recorded on a series of plaques in the old quarter. The Battle of Frigiliana Rock is remembered every year during the long established Feast of San Antonio with traditional music and dancing and a pilgrimage to Las Lomas de las Vacas.

**Nerja**, a bare 6km (4 miles) from Frigiliana, is no younger than any of the other coastal resorts but, apart from some highly complimentary Moorish poetry, has nothing to prove it. In the olden days it was known as *Narixa*, indicating that it had abundant spring water, and divided its time between weaving silk, fishing and growing sugar cane. Things might have continued like this if the Nerja Caves had not been discovered accidentally in 1959. Apparently a group of boys were exploring the profusion of caves scattered over the hills when they forced their way into a small grotto and found far more than they expected. Behind it were enormous caverns filled with stalactites and stalagmites, a few wall drawings and a variety of items such as tools and broken pottery from prehistoric times. When the archaeologists had completed their investigations the site was turned into a major tourist attraction. La Cascada was turned into an improvised theatre where ballets and concerts are staged during the season, and Nerja was soon on its way to becoming an important tourist resort.

Although there are still traces of the old village and plenty of sugar plantations all round, no silk has been produced for many years and there are few local fishermen. Apart from the seventeenth-century Church of San Salvador and the hermitage of the Virgen de las Angustias the only other well publicised attraction is the Balcón de Europa. This is a paved, finger-like promenade fringed with greenery that points out to the edge of the cliff with a magnificent view all along the coast. The hills behind are partly speckled with modern villas and there are some moderately tall buildings in the town including a choice of comfortable hotels in addition to the *parador*.

So far Nerja is bustling rather than brash. The little shops are predictable without being quaint and it is becoming increasingly difficult to park. However the resort has everything for an enjoyable seaside holiday such as small pleasure craft for hire, a 9-hole golf course, sandy beaches, underwater fishing and opportunities for shooting, climbing and walking up in the hills. Plans have been proposed for a massive tourist complex with everything from riding stables to a golf course, dry ski slope and casino. If this developer's dream becomes a reality then the little waterside hamlet of Maro will probably go the same way as all the other old fishing villages along the Málaga coast, which could be either a blessing or a disaster, depending on your point of view.

# 9
# *SEVILLA*

---

Sevilla, another landlocked region, is the largest province in Andalucía. It has four local neighbours — Huelva, Cádiz, Málaga and Córdoba and encroaches very slightly on Extremadura to the north. Roughly speaking it can be divided into three distinct areas, namely the Sierra Morena with its wooded hills, mines and hunting reserves and the southern pine and scrub encrusted Cordillera Subbética, separated by the much larger Depression of the Gualadquivir. The river makes a sedate entry from Córdoba in the north-east, curves gradually round in order to confer its favours on the capital and then continues southwards through marshes and rice paddies to lose itself in the Atlantic Ocean.

Throughout history Sevilla has owed most of its fame and fortune to the Guadalquivir. The Romans called it *Baetis* but this was changed to *Wadi el Kebir* (The Great Water), by the Arabs, a name that has altered less in its pronounciation than in its spelling during the intervening centuries. The fact that it is navigable for 81km (50 miles) or more enabled Sevilla to develop as an important maritime centre and today, with the help of constant dredging, it is still the only river port of any magnitude in Spain. A number of smaller tributaries such as the Genil, the Corbones and the Gualadimar increase the flow of this ancient waterway while at the same time providing irrigation for the citrus orchards and agricultural lands all along the banks.

Sevilla can trace its history back to Neolithic times and illustrates this with some pieces of pottery thought to have been fashioned in the Carmona area. Much more sumptuous discoveries in El Carambolo, on the outskirts of the capital, have given experts good reason for thinking that it may have been part of the fabled kingdom of *Tartessus* before the Carthaginians put in an appearance in about 500BC. They seem to have been on reasonably good terms with the

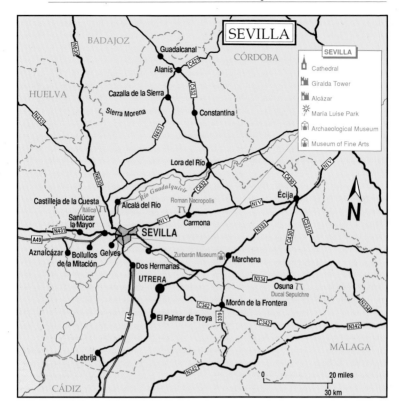

Greek and Phoenician traders who followed them but crossed swords with the Romans and were defeated at *Ilipa*, now Alcalá del Rio, in 206BC, or thereabouts. Julius Caesar chose a local Iberian settlement on the river as an ideal site for a new colony, thereby founding Sevilla and the administrative town of *Itálica*, 9km (6 miles) to the north-west.

The Visigoths and the Moors both added tremendously to the beauty and stature of Sevilla which, unlike Córdoba, then managed to survive the frequently debilitating attentions of the Catholic Monarchs after Ferdinand captured the city in 1248 and incorporated it into the kingdom of Castile. As the vast riches of the Indies began to pour into Spain most of the cargoes were diverted from Huelva to Sevilla, adding considerably to its wealth and prestige, but when this trade started to decline the city was quite unprepared for

*Sevilla: the Plaza de España*

*Sevilla: the Cathedral and Giralda Tower*

the dark days ahead. It was bedevilled by famine and epidemics, including the plague, but refused to surrender to its misfortunes. New buildings appeared and academics, writers, artists and musicians all played their part. The arrival of the railway and the steady growth of industry, coupled with the Latin American Exhibition of 1929, helped to put Sevilla back on its feet. Today it is busy and prosperous, the fourth largest city in Spain and the capital of Andalucía.

The province is very well placed as far as travellers are concerned. San Pablo Airport, on the main road to Carmona, is in regular contact with Madrid, Málaga and Barcelona and has additional services to Valencia, Lisbon and the Canary Islands. Trains run at frequent intervals to and from Madrid, Barcelona and the other provincial capitals of Andalucía, augmented by fleets of buses shuttling backwards and forwards to places as far apart as Ayamonte and Almería, Tarifa, Badajoz and Cádiz. Cars can be hired from at least a dozen different companies and there are plenty of taxi ranks and radio-taxis — although open horse-drawn carriages are by far the most pleasant way of touring the old quarter — and river boats operate summer schedules from a point near the Torre del Oro.

With the city as their central point, motorways lead off the newly constructed ring road in several different directions,. They provide fast links with Huelva to the west, Cadiz in the south, Málaga and Granda to the east and Córdoba on the main route to the north which, in turn, leads directly to Madrid. There are also well maintained highways to Jerez and northwards either through Zafra in Extramadura or across the Sierra de Aracena and into Portugal. A host of smaller, often scenic, roads provide access to all the outstanding places of interest scattered quite freely throughout the less frequented areas on either side of the Guadalquivir Valley, with one that follows the course of the river into Córdoba. Finally, a comprehensive network of little roads and byways offers some useful shortcuts as well as calling at isolated villages with no tourist attractions but plenty of atmosphere.

The city of Sevilla is inundated with hotels to suit every taste and pocket. By far the most outstanding at the moment is the Alfonso XIII, built for the Latin American Exhibition of 1929, surrounded by landscaped gardens, with every creature comfort and prices that reflect its five-star rating. There are plenty of four-star hotels and even more in the lower categories with dozens of little places, especially in the Barrio de Santa Cruz. Further afield Carmona has a reasonably historic *parador* and Alcalá de Guadaira a most acceptable hotel, but apart from these there is nothing really worth pinpointing elsewhere. For anyone towing a caravan or carrying a tent there is a campsite near the airport and two more in the vicinity of Dos Hermanas on the road to Cádiz.

So far **Sevilla** is a trifle short of top flight restaurants with the exception of those in one or two leading hotels and the Mesón del Moro, sited in a twelfth-century Arab bathhouse and much frequented by foreign visitors. This may be because so many people prefer the *tapas*, miniature dishes of every description that are served with drinks in the local bars. However there are plenty of other less exalted restaurants for people who prefer to eat in more conventional surroundings, including some which specialise in traditional dishes, Chinese food or even pizzas. The evenings bring a choice of theatres, concerts, ballet and cinemas, some dependent on the time of year, as well as flamenco shows, night clubs, discos and even bingo halls.

Apart from all the usual departmental stores and supermarkets, a great many little shops specialise in goods of all descriptions. Shopping in other towns and villages, where the local craftsmen often work from home, can prove to be an enjoyable pastime and frequently a less expensive one. Sporting enthusiasts can swim in any number of different pools or pass the time in boats on the rivers. The Betis Club is one of many places to play tennis, golf and riding are available at the Pineda Club and clay pigeon shooting at El Carambolo, while the Tablada Aeroclub has facilities for both flying and parachuting. For anyone whose inclinations lie more in the direction of spectator sports there is a fairly long horse racing season, bullfights and football matches at either of the two city stadiums. Elsewhere in the province it is also possible to join a shooting party or fish in one of the various lakes or rivers.

Regardless of these many diversions Sevilla is primarily a Mecca for sightseers, but it also has a darker side and one which visitors would do well to bear in mind. A great many impoverished families, attracted by the bright lights and the prospect of a job, live in stark highrise tenements on the city outskirts. Consequently it is unwise to wander about wearing a lot of jewellery, carrying a bulging handbag or with a wallet protruding invitingly from a trouser pocket. Nothing should ever be left on the seat of a car, even when it is moving. It is not unknown for youngsters on motorcycles to pull up alongside at a traffic light, lean over and smash a window if necessary to remove anything within reach and make off at speed.

Most people make for the cathedral, well-placed to one side of the old city with a splendid landmark in the shape of the Giralda Tower. The site was originally occupied by a mosque but this was pulled down in the fifteenth century to make way for the cathedral. It is the third largest Christian church in the world, after St Peter's in Rome and St Paul's in London, with some occasional reminders of its Moorish ancestry and plenty of things to see inside.

The interior is surprisingly dark and gloomy considering its size with an altarpiece intricately carved with scenes from the New Testament and saturated in gold. The Capilla Real, behind a protective grille presented by Carlos III in 1771, contains the tombs of Alfonso the Wise and his mother, Beatrice of Swabia. The remains of King Ferdinand, who recovered Andalucía from the Moors, was beatified and known thereafter as San Fernando, are preserved in a magnificent silver urn in the centre of the nave. This is opened twice a year, no doubt to prove once again that they have survived the ravages of time. Keeping watch over this saintly monarch is the Virgen de los Reyes, reputed to have been given to him by his cousin and fellow saint, King Louis of France. Meanwhile the coffins of Pedro the Cruel and his mistress, Doña Maria de Padilla, can be found in less august surroundings in the crypt.

Many of the little chapels are worth more than a passing glance, as are the paintings by Murillo, Zurbarán and Goya in the Sacristy of the Chalices and the enormous monstrance, complete with marble pillars, which is housed in the main sacristy. The cathedral treasure is rich and varied and includes the so-called Alfonsine Tables, a sword worn by King Ferdinand and a cross made from gold brought back by Columbus on one of his voyages to the West Indies. The Columbus monument with its four pall-bearers representing Castile, Aragon, León and Navarre, was added less than 100 years ago just inside the transept. Someone is certainly buried there but it seems increasingly unlikely that it is Cristóbal Colón.

The **Giralda Tower** was originally a minaret, built on Roman foundations by the Almohads 50 years or so before the Christians recaptured the city. In the early stages it had four gilded bronze apples at the top which were said to be visible to travellers who still had a full day's ride ahead of them. These were destroyed during an earthquake in the thirteenth century and were replaced by a belfry and a statue representing Faith which acts as a weathervane. Known as Giraldillo (something that turns) it eventually gave its name to the whole structure. It is a long but not over demanding climb to the top where there is a superb view over the city. The climb is by a ramp wide enough for two horses to pass each other. Back at ground level it is pleasant to wander through the Patio de los Naranjas, originally part of the mosque but now liberally planted with orange trees and attractively paved, with a Moorish fountain and some ancient walls

*Sightseeing in Sevilla by horse drawn carriage*

*Sevilla from the Giralda Tower*

and gateways.

The **Casa Lonja**, in the shadow of the Cathedral, was designed by Juan Herrera as a commercial Exchange in the reign of Philip II when business was booming. Later, as history, art and music took precedence over trade, the elegant old building was reconstituted as a home for the Archives of the Indies, a massive collection of documents, maps, letters and other paraphernalia concerned with the discovery and colonisation of the Spanish possessions in the New World.

The **Museum of Contemporary Art**, in the former chapel just next door, is only interested in paintings, drawings, sculptures, tapestries and other items produced by Spanish artists during the twentieth century. Its appeal is comparatively limited, which is also true of the small maritime museum housed in the Torre del Oro on the river bank a short distance away. This twelve-sided tower was quite probably covered with gilt tiles when it was constructed by the Moors in 1220 as part of the city defences. At one time a chain was strung across the water to control the river traffic but this, like the tower on the opposite bank to which it was attached, has now completely disappeared.

The old landing stages nearby, now the home of pleasure craft, were the scene of frantic activity whenever the silver fleets arrived back from the New World. They also witnessed the departure of Magellan, the Portuguese navigator who sailed in 1519 with a fleet of five Spanish ships to find the elusive sea route to India. Two years later he had rounded Cape Horn and reached the Philippines, only to be killed there in a fight with the local inhabitants. However his friend and companion, Juan Sebastian Elcano, a Basque from the village of Getaria on the Bay of Biscay, completed the voyage to become the first navigator to sail right round the world.

A block or two away from the Torre del Oro is the ancient **Hospital de la Caridad**, founded in the mid-seventeenth century and still providing a home for the impoverished sick and elderly. Its attendant chapel is extremely proud of Pedro Roldan's *Burial of Christ* over the high altar but a trifle undecided about two macabre paintings by Valdés Leal. It is said that Murillo, some of whose contributions to the chapel were appropriated by Napoleon, remarked that one had to hold one's nose when looking at them. It may not have been a very tactful observation by one artist about the works of his contemporary but it certainly is appropriate. The only other tourist attraction in the immediate vicinity is the attractive Maestranza bullring, dating from 1760, which has a river frontage and an enviable programme of annual events.

Adjacent to the cathedral is the **Alcázar** which, despite its name  and its appearance, owes practically nothing to the Moors. It was built on the ruins of an Arab palace by Pedro the Cruel in the latter half of the fourteenth century. The entrance is through a gateway off the Plaza del Triumfo and into the Patio de la Monteria, or Hunter's Court, overlooked by one of the most arresting Mudéjar façades in Spain. Beyond this are some superb little patios including the extremely decorative Patio de las Doncellas which, although named for the resident damsels, was nevertheless the centre round which the official life of the palace revolved. On the other hand the Dolls Court, or Patio de las Muñecas, was part of the private apartments where Pedro is believed to have murdered his brother, Don Fadrique.

Every successive Spanish ruler felt obliged to change the decor, although not as drastically as Charles V who tacked on a palace of his own. The Catholic Monarchs created the Casa de Contratación from which they could supervise the colonization of South and Central America. Here the Admiral's Apartments very properly contain the famous sixteenth-century altarpiece *The Virgen of the Navigators* and a model of the Santa María in which Columbus first set out across the Atlantic and discovered San Salvador. The gardens of the Alcázar  cover a more extensive area than the building itself. The lower section has both a labyrinth and a secluded pavilion built for Charles V which was apparently one of General Franco's favourite haunts when he spent an occasional holiday in the palace.

Outside the walls the Plaza de Catalina de Rivera is a promenade leading to the Jardines de Murillo which border on the Barrio de Santa Cruz. Another much shorter approach to this famous old Jewish quarter is through the Court of Flags and along a covered roadway into the Plaza del Doña Elvira where plays were once staged in the open air. In every direction a jumble of narrow streets edge their way past whitewashed houses. Every now and then they open out into a little square such as the lovely Cruz de Cerrajeria with its delicate wrought iron cross marking the spot where Murillo is buried.

A somewhat tortuous route past the Church of Santa Cruz leads to another oasis of religious and secular buildings comprising the San Ildefonso Church, the Church of San Esteban, the San Leandro Convent and the Casa de Pilatos. This fairly typical sixteenth century mansion with its grand staircase, beautiful tiles and statues of Minerva, was copied in part from the governor's residence in Jerusalem which caught the eye of Don Fadrique de Ribera, the Marqués de Tarifa, during a visit to the Holy Land. For the determined sightseer no less than a dozen other historic buildings, most of them

*The Torre del Oro, built by the Moors at Sevilla, now houses a small maritime museum*

*Birds enjoying a drinking fountain at the María Luisa Park, Sevilla*

churches, chapels or convents, are open to visitors on their way to the Macarena Gateway at one end of the rather sparse remains of the old encircling walls. An alternative route back again might well include the somewhat unprepossessing Alameda de Hercules with its weatherbeated statues of Julius Caesar and Hercules perched on their respective pillars. It was once a fashionable meeting place but has now, unfortunately, run to seed.

Anyone with some holiday shopping to do would probably find more than they bargain for in the area round the elongated Calle de la Feria where the second-hand dealers hold their Thursday markets. Another good place to bear in mind is in the Calle de las Sierpes, a winding pedestrian walk-way lined with ancient shops of all descriptions that look as though they have been in business for hundreds of years. It links La Campana with the Plaza de San Francisco, giving access to several places of interest on either side.

On one hand is El Salvador, Baroque, bulky and the largest church in Sevilla apart from the cathedral. It is within a stone's throw of the old university and the Lebrija Palace where a number of mosaics from *Itálica* have been preserved. On the opposite side is the Magdalena Church and beyond it the Museum of Fine Arts in the Plaza del Museo. The building was originally the Convento de la Merced and numbered among its occupants Tirso de Molina who created the famous character Don Juan. It claims to be the second most important picture gallery in Spain with works by El Greco, Zurbarán, Leal and Ribera among many others, with dozens of Murillos crammed into the old friary church. Some special items to look for are El Greco's portrait of his son, a particularly brutal carving of St Jerome by Torregiano who died in prison in Sevilla, and Zurbarán's *Miracle of St Hugo*, said by some people to be his masterpiece.

On the opposite side of the Barrio de Santa Cruz is the large and beautiful **María Luisa Park**. It started life as a faithful reproduction  of an English garden but had to be modified considerably for the Latin American Exhibition. A Frenchman called Forestier was given the job and redesigned the whole area.

Overlooking both the gardens and the river, the Palace of San Telmo is known primarily for its magnificent entrance, excessively carved and decorated with a great many pillars and statues and an occasional coat-of-arms. At various times it has been the home of the Dukes of Montpensier, a naval college and a rather grand school. Practically next door the university has taken possession of the massive eighteenth century Tobacco Factory second only in size to the Escorial and famous as the setting for Bizet's opera *Carmen*.

At the other end of the gardens there are two museums, both of which are exceptionally interesting. The furthest away is the **Arch-aeological Museum** which delves back into prehistory with fascinating exhibits unearthed at Carambolo and attributed to Tartessian craftsmen. The Romans are also well to the fore with contributions from the ruins of *Itálica*, including goddesses such as Venus and Diana and a selection of emperors, the most outstanding of which is Trajan. The Museum of Folk Art and Customs has considerably updated its outlook on life, concerning itself with everything from clothes to ceramics and agricultural implements to kitchen utensils as well as furniture, fabrics and musical instruments. It also provides house room for a number of exhibits connected with the festivities surrounding Holy Week and the April Fair.

Rivalling even the Tobacco Factory, the semi-circular Plaza de España completes the list of attractions in the María Luisa Park. The Palacio Centrale is less than 100 years old but it is very much in the Baroque style with domed towers, a liberal sprinkling of decorative tiles and an enormous colonnade reflected in the waters of its matching canal. There are milk white balustrades and colourful humpback bridges, a modicum of trees and small rowing boats for anyone who feels in need of a little gentle exercise.

Finally it would be a pity to leave the capital without crossing the Guadalquivir to visit the **Triana** district on the opposite bank, famous for both its ceramic factories and its flamenco bars. It was the haunt of seamen and other people connected with the river in its heyday and the fact that it was named after the Emperor Trajan suggests that it was founded in Roman times. The main architectural attraction is Santa Ana Church, built in the thirteenth century and the oldest parish church in the city. It stands facing the bullring across the water and slightly down stream from the Torre del Oro.

Sevilla is known throughout the world for its magnificent Holy Week fiesta and the April Fair that follows close on its heels. In the days leading up to Easter statues of Christ and the Virgin Mary are carried through the streets to the cathedral, accompanied by members of their brotherhoods wearing the sinister conical hats with slits for the eyes which call to mind the worse excesses of the Inquisition.

The April Fair is generally held some 2 weeks after Easter and lasts for about 6 days. It was originally a rural event devoted to livestock and cattle dealing but has widened its horizons considerably during the past 100 years or so. A temporary town of kiosks and pavilions springs up almost overnight, decorated with flowers, banners, flags and lanterns. In the late afternoon there are bull fights followed by more fun and fireworks that continue until dawn. Less well known, and admittedly not quite as colourful, are the Cavalcade of the Three Kings in January, the Corpus Christi processions, the Feast of the Virgen de los Reyes, the patron saint of the city, which is timed for August and the September bullfights that are all that remain of the Michaelmas Fair. Sandwiched in between are classical concerts, regattas on the river and several excursions to places of interest in the surrounding countryside.

Some 10km (6 miles) to the north of the capital are the ruins of **Itálica**, founded by Cornelius Scipio in 206BC as a fortified convalascent home for Roman soldiers. It gradually expanded into a city with 10,000 inhabitants, hundreds of villas, a large arena, temples and a theatre as well as the usual baths and a sophisticated drainage system. By the second century AD it had become one of the most important centres on the Iberian peninsula and the birthplace of two future emperors — Trajan and Hadrian.

After the collapse of the Roman Empire the buildings gradually disintegrated, a process that was ably assisted by the Lisbon earthquake of 1755. So far about one fifth of the city has been excavated, including the remains of the arena which could seat upwards of 20,000 spectators, the original theatre and a network of streets lined with the foundations of wealthy villas whose courtyards were covered with intricate mosaics. The theatre is more difficult to locate than the outer suburbs which climb up a slope near **Santiponse**, a rather dreary industrial town that was once part of *Itálica*. The best way to find it is to turn left before the Bar Parada on the road to the capital, after which it is about 200m down the hill. Other things to see before leaving the area are the *Itálica* museum and the Church of San Isidoro del Campo. It was founded in the early fourteenth century by Guzmán the Good, a legendary Spanish army commander who is buried there with his wife and younger son. As well as the carved altarpiece with its far from attractive figure of St Jerome there is a well proportioned cloister in the Mudéjar style. The cost of excavating *Itálica* is partly off-set by an international festival held there every year with performers from as far away as Hungary and Japan. There is also an annual marathon in January which attracts both experienced runners and amateur enthusiasts who join in partly with an eye on the prize money and partly just for fun.

The one or two places of interest to the west of Sevilla include **Castilleja de la Cuesta** with the palace of Hernán Cortéz where the intrepid conquistador is thought to have spent the last days of his life. It was built in the sixteenth century and, after a lot of restoration and refurbishing, was finally turned into a school. **Sanlúcar la Mayor** has no similar attractions to offer but it has made a point of preserving the remains of its original walls and three Mudéjar churches, all of which are mildly viewable. **Aznalcázar** weighs in with several eighteenth-century houses, a public fountain and the obligatory old church whereas **Bollullos de la Mitación** has some paintings by Zurbarán in the Church of St Martin and an Arab tower which stays more or less intact by leaning against the Hermitage of Cuatrovitas.

South of the capital the outlook is much the same. **Gelves** with its Baroque church and ruined palace vies for attention with **Dos Hermanas** which has the added advantage of a two-star motel, a couple of hostels, two campsites and direct access to both the motorway and the main road to Cádiz. Beyond the Guadalquivir Canal are the extensive rice fields of the river delta, divided up by small roads, the majority of which are quite unsuitable for motorists. Anyone who is determined to explore the marshes, whether for bird watching or any other reason, should keep strictly to the beaten tracks to avoid being trapped in the reeds or blundering into a patch of quicksand with no-one about to lend a helping hand.

Just short of the border **Lebrija** has converted a twelfth-century Almohad mosque into the very presentable Church of Santa María de la Oliva with domes and a well-matched tower that was added about 100 years ago. However, motorists in search of modern miracles should take the main road in preference to the motorway. After a pleasant run through fields of sunflowers, past a good selection of small wayside bars, there is a turning that doubles back to Utrera, passing within nodding distance of the hamlet of **El Palmar de Troya**. This is, apparently, a place much given to visions. Two young girls from the village said they saw the Virgin Mary in 1986 but Clemente Dominguez went a step further, insisting that stigmata appeared on his body after a similar experience. He proclaimed himself Pope Gregorio XVII, his followers built him a large church protected by encircling walls, he appointed his own clergy and created some new saints, namely General Franco and José Antonio, the founder of the Falange Party.

**Utrera** itself is fairly forgettable although it has a Roman bridge, some ancient walls, a ruined castle and various churches along with some elderly mansions. In addition it is not all that far from **Alcalá de Guadaira** which has restored its Arab castle and Mudéjar walls and rebuilt the Church of Santiago. From here a pleasant secondary road wanders off in a north-easterly direction through El Viso del Alcor to **Carmona** which certainly has quite a few things to boast about.

There is believed to have been a Neolithic settlement of some kind on the site, discovered first by the Greeks and then modernised and enlarged by the Romans until it achieved the status of an important walled city overlooking the plains of the Guadalquivir. The Arabs found it just as agreeable, adding several distinctive touches of their own, and even Pedro the Cruel paid it a certain amount of attention by extending the existing Alcázar where he later entertained John of Gaunt. It also made a convenient base for the Catholic Monarchs while they were launching their attacks against Granada. In much more recent times a comfortable *parador* was built inside the ancient castle with every modern facility as well as thoughtful touches such as arcades, a patio and a fountain to ensure that it made the most of the existing atmosphere.

The Sevilla Gate under its double Moorish arch provides the main entrance to the old city with its ancient palaces, little alleyways and churches filled with relics. The Santa Clara Convent allows visitors into its private chapel where the walls are hung with portraits of medieval women, whereas the Church of Santa María has a faintly Moorish air about it inspite of some fine fifteenth-century vaulting.

Although the town hall has a very interesting mosaic in the patio this is far from being the most important reminder of the Roman occupation. On the outskirts of the town is an ancient necropolis containing something like 800 different tombs, only about a third of which have been excavated. Most of them are little more than funeral chambers with stone niches for the urns but others are really quite palatial with paintings of people feasting and couches cut out of the rock. The tomb of the Servilii resembles a two-storey villa with a central pool, vaulted roof and a bed with Greek columns, probably designed for a woman. The Elephant Tomb takes its name from a decidedly world-weary statue at the entrance and consists of three large chambers, presumed to be dining halls, a kitchen and ample running water. There is also a local archaeological museum.

East of Carmona, on the main route to Madrid, is the town of **Ecija**, described by some people as the 'City of Towers' and by others, less interested in architecture, as 'The Furnace of Andalucía'. Certainly, like several other places in the area, it becomes oppressively hot in the summer but nevertheless it has been inhabited almost without a break since prehistoric times. The Romans thought enough of it to build an amphitheatre and several villas, now all but disappeared, while under Moorish rule it became the personal property of the caliphs of Córdoba. Some of the churches, like San Juan, San Gil and Santa Cruz, are very much the worse for wear although, for some strange reason, their belfries, overlaid with tiles, have survived almost intact and give the town its distinctive silhouette. Behind the remnants of its ancient walls there are quite a few decorative palaces and mansions, particularly in and around the Calle de los Caballeros, complimented by the Church of St James which was largely rebuilt after the ground underneath gave way in 1628.

The Guadalquivir runs more or less parallel to the Madrid highway but, apart from an occasional sleepy village, the road that accompanies it is fairly monotonous. However there is some attractive hilly country to the north with a couple of well-stocked dams much frequented by fishermen and enough game to keep the shooting fraternity happy. Most of the villages preserve something from their past, be it no more than a ruined castle, a restored church or an elderly hermitage. Even the most determined sightseer would be extremely unlikely to visit them all but anyone in search of out-of-the-way places might well be tempted to linger in **Constantina** with its old Moorish quarter and the remains of a medieval castle or **Cazalla de la Sierra** where the fifteenth century Carthusian monastery hides behind battered Arab walls. **Alanís**, on the other hand, has held on to part of an ancient castle, at least two Gothic hermitages and the Fountain of Santa María which was supplying the villagers with water while Charles V was busy adding his new palace to the Alhambra in Granada.

The whole area is very much mining country with **Guadalcanal** tucked up in one corner. If the name sounds familiar that is hardly surprising because the embattled island in the Pacific which figured so prominently during World War II was discovered by Pedro Ortega, a local resident who named it after his home town. Although it was once a Moorish outpost there are traces of much earlier inhabitants in several nearby prehistoric caves. In particular the  Santiago and San Francisco caves show traces of the families who sheltered in them during the Stone Age.

On the opposite side of the Guadalquivir, and particularly to the south of Lora del Rio, the famous Miura fighting bulls have free run of the extensive grasslands belonging to the local ranches. They are not particularly large as bulls go and look quite placid grazing in the distance, but it would be the height of folly to wander in amongst them. The mounted ranchers use long poles to handle their herds and even then they will seldom take any chances unless it is unavoidable.

**Marchena**, on the road which links the two main roads from Sevilla to Madrid and Málaga respectively, has preserved some ancient fortifications, three worthwhile churches and a good many  old mansions in addition to a pleasing square and a small museum devoted to Zurbarán. However **Osuna**, separated by flatish country and hundreds of olive trees, has rather more to recommend it. It is an elegant town which began life as a Roman military camp where, as far as one can see, nobody bothered about such refinements as arenas and under-floor heating. The Moors took a passing interest in it but, like their predecessors, failed to create anything of lasting value. In fact it was about 300 years before the university was founded in 1548. Ten years later the town leaped into the public eye when it became the family seat of the newly-created Dukes of Osuna, still today one of the most illustrious families in Spain.

This was the signal for an outbreak of feverish activity. Highly decorated palaces and mansions sprung up everywhere, especially in the Calle Sevilla and the Calle San Pedro, with gracious flower-filled patios hidden behind wrought iron grilles and heavy wooden doors. They were joined by a predictable number of convents and churches including the Convento de la Encarnación with its museum of sacred art and colourful seventeenth-century cloister smothered in tiles. The Collegiate Church, facing the world through a great, sculptured doorway, is by no means overwhelmed by its extravagant altarpiece incorporating four paintings by Ribera who was in the service of the Duke of Osuna when the latter was Viceroy of Naples in the early seventeenth century.

The **Ducal Sepulchre** heads the list of local attractions. It is reached by way of a patio surrounded by decorative marble arcades and is in two sections, the first a miniature church in its own right. At one time it was beautifully painted and adorned with gold leaf but this gradually disappeared under layers of soot, a legacy from thousands of tall, slow-burning candles. Above it is a separate vault, added in 1901, containing the coffins of leading members of the House of Osuna. Other tourist attractions include a small archaeological museum in the Torre del Agua which was once part of the ramparts, the chapter house and the former law courts that rejoice in the title of Antigua Audiencia.

On the way back to the capital, provided time allows, a secondary road branches off to the left, calling at **Morón de la Frontera** with its collection of elderly mansions, one of which stands in particularly lovely gardens. From here motorists who have an urge to explore fresh territory can carry on southwards to Coripe, a small border town where every typical whitewashed house appears to own at least one television aerial. Having literally taken the rough with the smooth on the way down from Morón de la Frontera, with rather more rough than smooth, the twisting, frequently scenic, road through the mountains comes as a pleasant surprise. After occasionally doubling back on itself to admire the view it wriggles down into Cádiz province to join the busy highway linking the Costa del Sol with the Costa de la Luz.

# Tips for Travellers

## Planning Your Visit

## Climate

The weather varies considerably between the mountains, the uplands and the coastal areas, as well as between winter and summer, but is hardly more predictable in Spain than it is anywhere else. The hottest months can be almost unbearable in parts of Andalucía, especially up on the plateau. Winters are especially hard on the higher ground and up in the Sierra Nevada which is never totally free of snow. There can be torrential rains and massive thunder storms, as well as high winds, grey days and drizzle but it is seldom very cold along the coastal belt.

*Weather Information: Málaga*

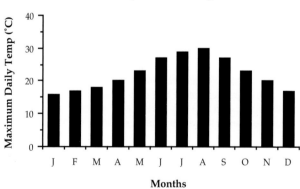

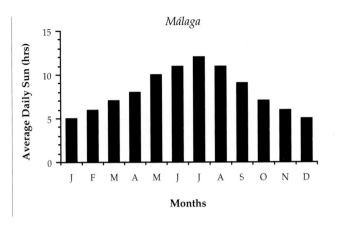

## Credit Cards

One or more of the most widely used credit cards, such as Access or Eurocard, American Express and Visa, are accepted by the majority of large hotels and restaurants, especially in the various resorts. The relevant logo is usually displayed in the window or at the reception desk but it is always as well to check in advance. So far not many garages will accept cards, nor will the majority of supermarkets, although the practice is gradually becoming more widespread along the coast.

## Currency

Any amount of foreign currency may be taken into Spain but only limited quantities of either *pesetas* or other currencies may be taken out again, unless it can be proved that any excess was brought in initially. It is wise to check the exact amounts.

## Customs Regulations

The customs regulations are similar to those in force
elsewhere in the EEC. If in any doubt it is as well to
check before leaving.

## Passports

A valid up-to-date passport is the only document
necessary for entry into Spain for the citizens of more
than fifty different countries including Britain, Canada
and the USA. Extensions are granted for visitors who
plan to stay for more than 3 months.

## Tourist Offices

**The Spanish National Tourist Office**
57-58 St James's Street
London SW1A 1LD
☎ 071 499 0901

**The British Consulate**
Duquesa de Parcent 8
Málaga
☎ (952) 21 48 88

**The United States Consular Agency**
Conjunto Sol Playa
Fuengirola
☎ (952) 47 48 91

**The Canadian Consulate**
Plaza de Malagueta 3
Málaga
☎ (952) 22 33 46

# *Travel*

### Air

Málaga has the only international airport in Andalucía but there are internal flights linking several provincial capitals such as Almería, Córdoba, Granada and Sevilla with Madrid, Barcelona and, in some cases, one or two other northern cities. Jerez takes care of the air traffic to Cádiz and there are regular services to Gibraltar from Gatwick and Tangier. Charter companies tend to home in on Málaga but also make use of some of the other local airports. Up-to-date information on fares and flight schedules is obtainable from the various airlines and from most travel agencies. A recent innovation is a 15 minute helicopter service between Málaga and Marbella.

### Cars, Motor Cycles and Bicycles

Car hire firms operate in all the main centres while in some resorts it is also possible to hire a motor cycle, a moped or a bicycle. The International Highway Code applies in Spain in exactly the same way as it does in other European countries. No-one under 16 is allowed to drive at all, apart from cyclists of course, and 18 is the minimum age for taking anything over 75cc out on the roads. Crash helmets are obligatory and motorists must wear seat belts and be adequately insured. Anyone who is used to driving on the left hand side of the road should be particularly careful at roundabouts, bearing in mind that traffic from the right always has priority unless the major route has the official right of way. Visitors who intend to use their own cars in Spain would be wise to have a word with their own motoring organisations before leaving because there are other regulations which must be observed. Third party insurance is compulsory in Spain and full comprehensive cover is advisable. Motorists bringing their own cars into the country should always check with their own insurance companies before setting out. Cars hired in Spain do not usually have insurance cover for entering Gibraltar, so motorists should check beforehand.

The condition of the roads in Andalucía varies enormously. There are motorways from Huelva via Sevilla and Córdoba to Madrid, from Sevilla to Cadiz and from Sevilla round Granada to Baza. Another branches off at Antequera for Málaga where it joins the coastal motorway linking Rincón de la Victoria with Algeciras. Most of the main routes are well maintained and present very few problems but some secondary roads can spring an odd surprise or two in the form of potholes and damaged verges, especially where there is a lot of heavy traffic. The minor roads are problematical but there is seldom anything that cannot be handled with due care and attention. Fuel is available nearly everywhere but there can be the odd exception, so it is as well to keep the tank filled up, especially before heading for one of the more inaccessible areas. Parking can be a problem almost everywhere and nothing should ever be left on the seats, although this does apply more to large towns than to small villages. It is also wise to carry a good map such as the ones produced by Michelin but the tourist offices can usually be relied upon to provide their excellent *Mapa de Communicaciones* as well as detailed maps of their own towns.

**Buses, Coaches and Taxis**
For anyone without a car the best way of seeing Andalucía is by bus. Dozens of different companies operate regular services between all the different towns and villages and, for the most part, they are comfortable, reliable and run at frequent intervals. Long distance coaches provide a comprehensive network of routes to all parts of the country while several tour operators in the main holiday resorts lay on special trips to places of outstanding interest. Local schedules are usually posted up in towns along the major routes such as the coastal highway from Málaga, but it is often easier to get all the details from the nearest tourist office because some of the bus stations can be a trifle inaccessible. Taxis are plentiful and not too expensive. They all have meters but are allowed to charge extra for things like luggage, night calls and journeys beyond the city limits when it is

advisable to agree the fare in advance. In addition to picking up a car on one of the official ranks it is often possible to flag down a passing cab or, failing that, telephone for a radio taxi. In towns like Sevilla, Córdoba and Granada the most enjoyable way of touring the old quarters is to hire a horse-drawn carriage and leave the driver to worry about the traffic.

**Rail**

All the major cities and several of the larger centres in Andalucía are linked by rail, both with each other and with more distant parts of the country. The best way to travel, apart from the luxury Trans Europe Express, is by using the Talgo trains which are fast and comfortable or the similar TER. However some of the other services can be exceedingly slow and frustrating. Every city has a RENFE travel office which will supply information and sell tickets in advance, thereby avoiding any confusion at the station. There are a number of special services and discounts on offer but anyone without a good command of the language may have some difficulty in finding out exactly what is available.

## When You Are There

## Dress

The rules governing dress in Spain have been considerably relaxed in recent years. Topless sunbathing is common but you must cover up when you leave the beach. Casual clothes are quite acceptable in seaside hotels and restaurants but more up-market establishments expect their guests to dress accordingly. Care should be taken not to give offence when visiting churches, convents or monasteries.

## Electricity

The usual voltage is 220 or 225 AC although there are some places which still operate on 110 or 125 AC.

Adapters will be needed by those people who do not use continental two-pin plugs at home.

## Health Care

Visitors covered by British National Insurance can expect to benefit under the Spanish Health Service, however it is wise to have additional insurance, which is essential for everybody else. American and Canadian visitors will need to check the validity of their personal health insurances to guarantee they are adequately covered. All the usual services are available and the pharmacies, identified by a green cross, can usually deal with minor problems or suggest the best place to go for assistance.

## Markets

Most of the towns and villages have open-air markets, the majority of which are purely functional and give good value for money. Others may be more specialised, especially in the main tourist areas, and ready to bargain over the more expensive items.

## Metrication

1 kilo (1,000 grams) — 2.2lb
1 litre         — $1^3/_4$ pints
4.5 litres    — 1 gallon
8km           — 5 miles

## Opening Hours

Most of the banks in Andalucía are open 6 days a week from 9am-2pm on weekdays and 9am-1pm on Saturdays. However the smaller branches may close earlier on Saturdays while some banks in the larger resorts stay open on weekdays until 2.30pm. Shops, with the exception of supermarkets, close for a 3 or 4 hour lunch at about 1.30pm and usually stay open until 7.30pm or even 8pm.

# Public Holidays

Spain usually has eleven or twelve official holidays but even some of these are open to negotiation. A town may decide to swap one of them for a more convenient date while most places have an additional day off to honour a local saint or commemorate some important occasion. Official public holidays are:

New Year's Day
6 January (Epiphany)
Maundy Thursday (Thursday before Easter)
Good Friday
1 May (Labour Day)
Corpus Christi
25 July (Santiago, or St James's Day)
15 August (Ascension Day)
1 November (All Saints Day)
6 December (Constitution Day)
8 December (Immaculate Conception)
25 December

# Souvenirs

Souvenirs in Andalucía vary; some of them are very ordinary and hardly worth bothering about while others are certainly worth their weight in *pesetas*, particularly if they are made by local craftsmen and not mass produced. Among the many things to look out for are blankets and ponchos in Cádiz, embroidered mantillas and other hand embroidered articles in Granada, silk shawls in Sevilla and leather goods, particularly in Córdoba. Wrought iron, basketwork of all descriptions and some filigree jewellery can be most attractive while traditional copper, bronze and ceramics make most acceptable presents. There are a good many antique shops in the main cities but the owners are well aware of the value of their stock.

## Telephones

Direct calls can be made from all the provincial capitals
and many of the main tourist resorts. For international
calls dial 07 and wait for the higher tone, then 44 for
Britain followed by the STD number but remember to
drop the 0 at the beginning. For the USA and Canada the
identification number is 1.

## Tipping

A service charge is often but not invariably added to a
bill whereas the equivalent of VAT is automatically
included. However it is customary to leave a tip unless
the food or the service has been unsatisfactory. It is not
necessary to tip in bars but taxi drivers and people
giving a personal service such as guides, usherettes,
porters and cloakroom attendants should always receive
something.

# FURTHER INFORMATION

## Places of Interest

Apart from the main museums and places of artistic or historical interest in the larger cities it is almost impossible to predict future opening and closing times. However, as a general rule, they all close for lunch and stay open slightly longer on summer evenings than they do in winter. Some churches are open only for services but the sacristan is usually somewhere close by and will invariably produce the key in return for a modest contribution to the church funds. Some outlying caves and ancient ruins have their own caretakers, who may also act as guides. Here again some tangible form of appreciation is expected even if it is not obligatory. It is a good idea to check with the tourist office, especially if a journey is involved, but it is fairly safe to assume that most places are closed on Mondays.

### 1 — ALMERÍA

**Almería**
*Alcazaba*
Open: 10am-2pm and 4-9pm. In winter 9am-1pm and 3-6.30pm.

*Cathedral*
Open: 8.30am-12noon and 5.30-8pm.

*Centro de Rescate de la Fauna Sahariana*
May only be visited with permission from the main office of the centre in the city, near the tourist office.

*Mini Hollywood*
Open: daily in the summer but frequently closed out of season. Enquire from the tourist office.

### 2 — CÁDIZ

**Cádiz**
*Cathedral and Museum*
Museum open: 10am-1pm and 5-7pm March to October. 10am-1pm and 4-6pm November to February. Closed Saturday afternoons, Sundays and holidays. Cathedral open: 9.30am-6.30pm.

*Church of San Felipe Neri*
Open: during services and on request.

*Municipal Museum*
Calle Santa Inés
Open: 9.30am-1.30pm and 5-9pm. 10am-2pm on Sundays.

*Museums of Fine Arts and Archaeology*
Plaza de Mina
Open: 9am-2pm and 5-8pm. Closed on Mondays.

**Jerez de la Frontera**
*Archaeological Museum*
Plaza de la Anunción

*Bodegas*
Open: on weekday mornings except in August. Enquire at the respective reception offices.

*Cartuja de la Defensión*

*Clock Museum*
Palacio de la Atalaya
Calle Cervantes

*Equestrian Training School*
Recreo de las Cadenas Palace

*Flamenco and Flamencology Museum*
Calle Quintos
All the above open most mornings and afternoons. For specific times enquire at the town hall.

*Museum of the Horse and the Wine*
Recreo de las Cadenas Palace

## Arcos de la Frontera
*Carpet Factory*
Open: during working hours.

*Church of San Pedro*
Facing the Calle Núñez de Prado
If closed enquire from the sacristan.

*Church of Santa María de la Anunción*
Plaza de España
If closed enquire from the sacristan.

## Tarifa
*Castle*
Guided tours 9.30am-1pm Fridays and Saturdays.

## Baelo Claudia
Roman ruins near Tarifa
Enquire at the local café whose owner also acts as guide.

## 3 — CÓRDOBA

## Córdoba
*Mosque, Cathedral and the Treasure*
Open: 10.30am-1.30pm and 3.30-7pm April to September. Otherwise 10.30am-1.30pm and 5-7pm.

*Archaeological Museum*
Plaza Jerónimo Páez
Open: 10am-2pm and 6-8pm May to September; 10am-2pm and 5-7pm October to April. Closed Sunday afternoons and Mondays.

*Calahorra Tower*
Open: 9.30am-2pm and 5-7pm. Closed Sunday evening and Monday. Multivision shows 11am, 12noon, 1pm, 3pm and 4pm.

*Castle of the Catholic Monarchs*
Open: 9am-1.30pm and 5-8pm. Gardens floodlit 10pm-midnight May to September. Closed Mondays.

*Fine Arts Museum*
Plaza del Potro
Open: 10am-1.30pm and sometimes in the late afternoon.

*Julio Romero de Torres Museum*
Plaza del Potro
Open: 10am-1.30pm.

*Municipal Museum*
Plaza de Maimonides
Open: 9.30am-1.30pm and 4-7pm. Closed Mondays.

*Synagogue*
Calle Judio
Open: 10am-2pm and 6-8pm May to September; 10am-2pm and 5-7pm October to April; 10am-1.30pm Sundays and holidays. Closed Mondays.

*Viana Palace*
Plaza Don Gome
Open: 9am-2pm June to September; 10am-1pm and 4-6pm October to May; 10am-2pm Sundays and holidays. Closed Wednesdays.

**Medina Azahara**
About 10km (6 miles) west of
Córdoba
Open: 10am-2pm and 6-8pm May
to September; 10am-2pm and 4-
6pm October to April; 10am-
1.30pm Sundays and holidays.
Closed Mondays.

**Montilla**
*Casa del Inca*
Capitan Alonso de Vargas 3
Open: 10am-1.30pm and 5-9pm.

**4 — GIBRALTAR**

*Cable Car*
Grand Parade to the summit.

*Casino*
Gaming tables open 8pm, 4pm
Sundays and holidays. Slot
machines open 9am.

*Ceremony of the Keys*
Casemates Square
For precise dates enquire at the
tourist office.

*Changing the Guard*
At The Convent
10.20am Tuesdays.

*Crazy Golf*
Open: 10am-6pm.

*The Galleries*
Open: 10am-7pm summer. 10am-
5.30pm winter.

*Gibraltar Museum*
Open: 10am-6pm Monday to
Saturday.

*Moorish Castle*
Open: 10am-7pm summer. 10am-
5.30pm winter.

*St Michael's Cave*
Open: 10am-7pm summer; 10am-
5.30pm winter. *Son et Lumière* 11am

and 4pm. Lake can be viewed by
arrangement.

*Scenic Tours*
For specific times ☎ 79200 or 76151 or
76070 or 70027. Or enquire from the
hall porter at the hotel.

**5 — GRANADA**

**Granada**
*Alhambra and Generalife*
Open: 9.30am-8.30pm May to August;
9.30am-6pm September to April;
9.30am-5.30pm Sundays. Interior
floodlit 10pm to midnight Wednesdays and Saturdays in summer, 8-
10pm Saturdays in winter.

*Arab Baths*
Carrera del Darro 31
Open: daily. For specific times
enquire at the tourist office.

*Archaeological Museum*
Casa de Castil
Carrera del Darro 41
Open: 10am-2pm and 6-10pm. Times
may be subject to alteration.

*Capilla Real*
Adjoining the cathedral
Open: 10.30am-1pm and 4-7pm
March to September; 10.30am-1pm
and 3.30-6pm October to February.

*Carmen de los Martires*
Below the Alhambra
Open: on Sundays.

*Carthusian Monastery*
On the road to Alfacar
Open: 10.30am-1pm and 4-7pm
March to September; 10.30am-1pm
and 3.30-6pm October to February.

*Church of San Juan de Dios*
Calle de San Juan de Dios
Church and museum open: 10am-
1pm and 4-6pm.

*Church and Monastery of San Jerónimo*
Calle de López Argueta
Open: 10am-1pm and 4-6.30pm in summer; 10am-1.30pm and 3-6pm in winter. Opens at 11.30am on Sundays and holidays.

*Convento de Santa Catalina de Zafra*
Carrera del Darro 43
Open: for masses.

*Corral del Carbón*
Open: during shopping hours.

*Home of Manuel de Falla*
In the Antequeruela
Open: on request. Closed Mondays.

*Huerta de San Vincent*
Calle Arabial
Open: by arrangement.

*Palace of the Madraza*
Opposite the Capilla Real
Can sometimes be seen on request.

*Museum of History and Handicrafts*
Casa de los Tiros
Plaza del Padre Suárez
Being refurbished. Enquire at the tourist office in the same building.

**Guadix**
*Church of Saint Anne*
Open: for mass. Otherwise enquire at Granada tourist office.

**Baza**
*Alcazabar*
Open: daily.

*Cathedral*
Open: for mass.

**Huéscar**
Parish church may be visited on request.

**Iznalzoz**
*Cave of the Water*
Open: only by special arrangement.

**Pinar**
*Castle*
Open: all day.

*Cave of the Carihuela*
Open: only by arrangement.

**Montefrío**
*Church of St Mary*
Open: all day.

*Church of the Incarnation*
Open: mornings only.

*Hipo-Nova*
Open: all day.

**Moclin**
*Castle*
Open: all day.

**Almuñécar**
*Castle*
Open: all day.

**Lanjarón**
Spa open: June to October.

**Trevélez**
*Drying Sheds*
Open: during working hours on request.

**Capileira**
*Alpujarran Folk Museum*
Enquire for the key at the town hall.

**Solynieve**
Open: mainly November to May.
*Parador* open: throughout the year.

**6 — HUELVA**

**Huelva**
*Archaeological Museum*
Alameda Sundheim 13
Open: daily 10am-2pm and 5-7pm.

Closed Mondays and Sunday afternoons.

**Ayamonte**
Ferry services to Portugal daily. Customs open: 8am to midnight in summer and 9am-9pm in winter.

**Monasterio de la Rábida**
Guided tours 10am-1.30pm and 4-8pm. Closed Mondays in winter.

**Moguer**
*Juan Ramón Jiménez Museum*
Open: 10am-2pm and 4-8pm; 10am-2pm and 4.30-8.30pm in summer.

*Museum of Religious Art*
Open: 11am-1pm and 4-6pm. Closed Sunday and Monday afternoons.

*Parque Nacional de Doñana*
Conducted tours. For details apply to the tourist office in Huelva, Sevilla or telephone the information centre in Matalscañas.
☎ (955) 43 04 32 or the information centre at La Rocina ☎ (955) 406140

**Aracena**
Gruta de las Maravillas.
Guided tours of the caves 11am to 7pm June to September, October to May 10am and 6pm.

# 7 — JAÉN

**Jaén**
*Cathedral*
The relic of St Veronica is shown to the congregation on Fridays after mass at 11am and 5pm.

*Cathedral Museum*
Open: 8.30am-1.30pm and 4.30-7pm. 11am-1pm Fridays, Saturdays and Sundays. These hours may be extended during the season.

*Provincial Museum*
Paseo de la Estación 29
Open: 10am-2pm and 4-7pm. Closed on Mondays and holidays.

**Andújar**
*Church of Santa María*
Open: 11am-1pm and 6-9pm. Closed from November to early April.

**La Carolina**
*Archaeological Museum*
Cervantes 8
No specified hours.

**Linares**
*Provincial Museum*
Yanguas Jiminez. No specified hours.

**Baeza**
*Cathedral*
If closed enquire at the tourist office.

*Palace and University*
If closed enquire at the tourist office.

**Úbeda**
*Casa de las Cadenas*
Open: during office hours. Murals can be seen in the mornings, 9am-2pm, on request.

*Church of El Salvador*
If closed apply to the sacristan, first door on the right in the Calle Francisco de los Cobos.

*Local Museum*
Cervantes and the Plaza Primero de Mayo
Open: 9am-1.30pm and 4-7pm. Closed Mondays.

**Quesada**
*Zabaleta Museum*
Plaza de Coronación 10
Open: 12noon to 2pm.

## Málaga

*Alcazaba and Archaeological Museum*
☎ 21 60 05
Open: 10am-1pm and 5-8pm.
Closed Sundays.

*Cathedral*
Open: 10am-1pm and 4-5.30pm.

*Museo de Semana Santa*
Plaza de San Pedro
☎ 31 23 94
Open: 10am-1pm and 4-7pm.
Closed Sundays and national
holidays.

*Museum of Fine Arts*
Calle San Agustin 6
☎ 21 83 82
Open: 10am-1pm and 5-8pm in
summer; 10am-1pm and 4-7pm in
winter. Closed Sunday afternoon
and Monday.

*Museum of Popular Art*
Paseo de Santa Isabel 7
☎ 21 71 37
Open: 10am-1pm and 5-8pm in
summer; 10am-1pm and 4-7pm in
winter. Closed on Sunday afternoon, Mondays and holidays.

*Picasso Museum*
No times available at the moment.
Enquire from the tourist office.

*Roman Auditorium*
Open: all day.

## Torremolinos
*Waxworks Museum*
Carretera de Cádiz
Open: 10am-10pm.

## Benalmádena Costa
*Tivoli World Amusement Park*
Arroyo la Mie
☎ 44 18 96 and 44 28 48

Open: daily throughout the season
but usually closed in winter.

## Benalmádena Pueblo
*Archaeological Museum*
Open: 10am-2pm and 5-8pm in
summer; 10am-2pm and 4-7pm in
winter. Closed Mondays and
holidays.

## Fuengirola
*Zoo*
Camino de Santiago
☎ 47 31 56
Open: 10am-2pm and 5-9pm in
summer; 9am-1pm and 3-7pm in
winter; 10am-9pm Saturdays,
Sundays and holidays.

## Marbella
*Municipal Museum*
Plaza de los Naranjos
☎ 77 46 38
Open: 11am-1pm and 5-8pm.
Closed Saturdays and Sundays.

## Estepona
Fish market operates in the early
morning.

## Ronda
*Arab Baths*
Open: 10am-1pm and 4-7pm.
Closed Sunday afternoons and
Mondays.

*Bullring and Museum*
Open: 10am-2pm and 4-7pm.

*Church of Santa María la Mayor*
If closed apply to the sacristan.

## Cueva de la Pileta
Open: 10am-8pm. If closed contact
the guide who lives nearby. It is as
well to take a torch if possible.

## Churriana
Times for the different gardens
vary. Check with the tourist office.

**Carratraca**
Spa operates from mid-June to mid-October.

**Antequera**
*Cueva de Menga and Cueva del Viera*
Open: 10am-1pm and 4-8pm in summer; 10am-1pm and 2-6pm in winter.

*Cueva del Romeral*
Collect the key from the sugar factory.

*Municipal Museum*
Open: 10am-1.30pm; 11am-1pm Sundays. Closed Mondays.

**El Torcal**
A tour of the area takes anything from 1 to 3 hours.

**Archidona**
*Hermitage of the Virgin*
Open: 9am-2pm and 3-7pm.

**Nerja**
*Caves*
Open: 9.30am-9pm May to mid-September. Otherwise 10am to 1.30pm and 4-7pm.

## 9 — SEVILLA

**Sevilla**
*Alcázar*
Open: 9am-1pm and 3-5.30pm. 9am-1pm only Saturdays, Sundays and holidays.

*Archaeological Museum*
Plaza de America
In the María Luisa Park
☎ 23 24 05
Open: 10am-2pm. Closed Mondays and some holidays.

*Casa de Pilatos*
Open: 9am-6pm. Upper floor open 10am-1pm and 3-6pm. Closed

Saturday afternoon and Sunday.

*Casa Lonja*
Av de la Constitución
For research only ☎ 22 51 58
Open: 10am-1pm Monday to Friday

*Cathedral and Giralda Tower*
Open: 10.30am-1pm and 3.30-5.30pm; 10.30am-1pm and 4-6pm in winter. Sundays 10.30am-1pm.

*Museum of Contemporary Art*
Adjacent to the Casa Lonja
☎ 21 58 30
Open: 10am-2pm and 4-7pm. Closed Saturday and Sunday afternoons and on Monday

*Museum of Folk Arts and Customs*
Plaza de America
In the María Luisa Park
☎ 23 25 76
Open: 10am-2pm. Closed Mondays and some holidays.

*Torre del Oro and the Maritime Museum*
Paseo de Colón
☎ 22 24 91
Open: 10am-2pm. 10am-1pm Sundays and holidays. Closed on Mondays.

**Itálica**
Near Santiponce.
Open: 9am-6.30pm in summer; 9am-5pm October to February; 9am-3pm Sundays. Closed Mondays.

**Carmona**
*Roman Necropolis*
☎ 14 08 11
Open: 10am-2pm and 4-6pm. Closed Mondays and holidays.

**Marchena**
*Zurbarán Museum*
No specific hours.

**Osuna**
*Ducal Sepulchre*
Guided tours 10am-1.30pm and 4-7.30pm. 10am-1.30pm and 3-6.30pm October to May. Closed Mondays.

# Tourist Information Offices

## 1 — ALMERÍA

**Almería**
Calle Hermanos Machado 4
In the Municipal Buildings
☎ 23 47 05

## 2 — CÁDIZ

**Cádiz**
Tourist Office
Plaza de Mina
☎ 22 48 00 or 21 13 13

Provincial Tourist Office
Plaza de España
☎ 22 48 00

El Puerto de Santa María
Municipal Tourist Office
Calle Guadalete
☎ 86 31 45

**Algeciras**
Tourist Office
Avenida de la Marina
☎ 60 09 11 or 65 67 61

## 3 — CÓRDOBA

**Córdoba**
Bureau of the Junta de Andalucía
Hermanos González Murga 13
☎ 47 12 35

City Council Tourist Information Centre
Plaza de Juda Levi in Judería
☎ 29 07 40

## 4 — GIBRALTAR

**Cathedral Square**
☎ 76400

**The Piazza**
John Mackintosh Square
☎ 76400

**Frontier Office**
☎ 76400

**Air Terminal**
☎ 76400

## 5 — GRANADA

**Granada**
Casa de los Tiros
Calle Pavaneras 19
☎ 22 10 11 or 22 10 22

## 6 — HUELVA

**Huelva**
Vázquez López 5
☎ 24 50 92

**Matalascañas**
In the Urbanización Playa de Matalascañas

## 7 — JAÉN

**Jaén**
Arquitecto Berges 1
☎ 22 27 37

Paseo de la Estación 30
☎ 22 92 00

**Baeza**
Plaza de los Leones
☎ 74 04 44

**Úbeda**
Bajos del Ayuntamiento
☎ 75 08 97

## 8 — MÁLAGA

**Málaga**
Municipal Tourist Office
Pasaje de Chinitas
☎ 22 94 21 and 22 79 07

**Antequera**
Calle Nájera 7
☎ 84 21 80

**Alhaurin el Grande**
Municipal Tourist Office
Edificio Mercado de Mayoristas
☎ 49 09 13 and 49 00 58

**Benalmadena Costa**
Municipal Tourist Office
Carretera de Cádiz
☎ 44 13 63

Tourist Office of the Junta de
Andalucía
☎ 44 24 94

**Estepona**
Paseo Maritimo
☎ 80 09 13

**Fuengirola**
Municipal Tourist Office
Plaza de España
☎ 47 95 00

**Marbella**
Municipal Tourist Office
Miguel Cano 1
☎ 77 14 42

**Nerja**
Municipal Tourist Office
Balcón de Europa
☎ 52 15 31

**Ronda**
Tourist Office of the Junta de
Andalucía
Plaza de España
☎ 87 12 72

**Torre del Mar**
Municipal Tourist Office
Avenida de Andalucia 110
☎ 54 11 04

**Torremolinos**
Tourist Office of the Junta de
Andalucía
La Nogalera
☎ 38 15 78

Municipal Tourist Office
Calle Gueteria
☎ 38 15 78

**Torrox Costa**
Municipal Tourist Office
Calle Franco 1
Carretera de Almería-Conejito
☎ 53 02 25

## 9 — SEVILLA

**Sevilla**
Provincial Tourist Information
Office
Av de la Constitución 24
☎ 21 10 91 or 22 56 53

Tourist Information Office
Av de la Constitución 21
☎ 22 14 04

Municipal Information Centre
Paseo de las Delicias
☎ 23 44 65

# *INDEX*

# Visitor's Guides

*Itinerary based guides for independent travellers*

**MPC**

*America:*
America South West
California
Florida
Orlando & Central
   Florida
USA

*Austria:*
Austria
Austria: Tyrol &
   Vorarlberg

*Britain:*
Cornwall & Isles of
   Scilly
Cotswolds
Devon
East Anglia
Hampshire & Isle of
   Wight
Kent
Lake District
Scotland: Lowlands
Somerset, Dorset &
   Wiltshire
North Wales &
   Snowdonia
North York Moors,
   York & Coast
Northern Ireland
Northumbria
Peak District
Treasure Houses of
   England
Yorkshire Dales &
   North Pennines

Canada
Czechoslovakia

Denmark
Egypt

*France:*
Champagne &
   Alsace-Lorraine
France
Alps & Jura
Brittany
Burgundy
Dordogne
Loire
Massif Central
Normandy
Normandy Landing
   Beaches
Provence & Côte
   d'Azur

*Germany:*
Bavaria
Black Forest
Northern Germany
Rhine & Mosel
Southern Germany

*Greece:*
Greece (mainland)
Athens &
   Peloponnese

Holland
Hungary
Iceland & Greenland

*India:*
Delhi, Agra & Jaipur
Goa

Ireland

*Islands:*
Corsica
Crete
Cyprus
Gran Canaria
Guernsey,
   Alderney & Sark
Jersey
Madeira
Mallorca, Menorca,
   Ibiza &
   Formentera
Malta & Gozo
Mauritius, Rodrigues
   & Reunion
Rhodes
Sardinia
Seychelles
Tenerife

*Italy:*
Florence & Tuscany
Italian Lakes
Northern Italy
Southern Italy

Norway
Peru
Portugal

*Spain:*
Costa Brava
   & Costa Blanca
Northern & Central
   Spain
Southern Spain
   & Costa del Sol

Sweden
Switzerland
Turkey

**MPC Visitor's Guides** are available through all good bookshops. Free catalogue available upon request from Moorland Publishing Co Ltd, Moor Farm Road West, Ashbourne, Derbyshire DE6 1HD, ☎ 0335 344486.

**Mail Order** In case of local difficulty, you may order direct (quoting your VISA/Access number) from Grantham Book Services on ☎ 0476 67421. Ask for the cash sales department. There is a small charge for postage and packing.